USING
COMMON WORSHIP:
Funerals

A Practical Guide to the New Services

R Anne Horton

CHURCH HOUSE
PUBLISHING

Church House Publishing
Church House
Great Smith Street
London SW1P 3NZ

ISBN   0 7151 2005 0

Published 2000 by Church House Publishing and *Praxis*

Telephone   020 7898 1557
Fax   020 7898 1449
Email   *copyright@c-of-e.org.uk*

Printed by   The Cromwell Press Ltd, Trowbridge, Wiltshire

Typeset in   11pt Sabon and 11.5pt Gill Sans
               by Pioneer Associates (Graphic) Ltd, Perthshire

Cover design
by   Silver Fish Creative Marketing

Contents

Part 3: Making the services work for us

In affectionate memory of those many friends and fellow Christians whose living and dying is woven into the pages of this book.

What is *Praxis*?

Praxis was formed in 1990, sponsored by the Liturgical Commission of the Church of England, the Alcuin Club, and the Group for the Renewal of Worship (GROW). It exists to provide and support liturgical education in the Church of England.

Its aims are:

- to enrich the practice and understanding of worship in the Church of England;

- to serve congregations and clergy in their exploration of the call to worship;

- to provide a forum in which different worshipping traditions can meet and interact.

The name *Praxis* comes from the Greek word for action. It emphasizes our practical concerns and conveys our conviction that worship is a primary expression of the Christian faith.

Praxis runs an annual programme of day conferences and residential workshops around the country, organized either centrally or by *Praxis* regions (informal networks of diocesan liturgical committees).

You can find out more about *Praxis* from our web site: www.sarum.ac.uk/praxis/

For a copy of the *Praxis* programme and details of how to affiliate, contact the *Praxis* office:

Praxis
St Matthew's House
20 Great Peter Street
LONDON
SW1P 2BU
Tel: 020 7222 3704
Fax: 020 7233 0255
Email: praxis@stmw.globalnet.co.uk

Foreword

Those who produced the *Common Worship* services wanted to provide liturgical resources that encourage worshipping communities to take account of the pastoral needs of the congregation and the mission imperative of worship that engages with the surrounding culture.

The synodical process has, rightly, focused on the texts, the structures and the rubrics. But the services will only come to life and reach their potential as living encounters with God in the nitty-gritty of worship in parish churches, hospital and prison chapels, school halls and other centres of worship. *Praxis* was set up by the Liturgical Commission in partnership with The Group for the Renewal of Worship (GROW) and the Alcuin Club to foster just such a practical approach to liturgy – working at grass roots level to support real churches who are seeking to make their regular worship better. *Praxis* has been running training events and courses to this end for ten years and it is a great step forward to see the combination of deeper understanding and better practice coming together in print.

The *Using Common Worship* series is a creative partnership between *Praxis* and Church House Publishing which will help all of us to make the most of *Common Worship*. Each volume bridges the gap between the bare texts and the experience of using those texts in worship. Full of practical advice, backed up with the underlying thinking from members of the Liturgical Commission, these books will be a valuable tool to put alongside the *Common Worship* volumes on the shelves of every worship leader in the Church of England.

✠ *David Sarum*
Chairman of the Liturgical Commission

Acknowledgements

The publisher gratefully acknowledges permission to reproduce copyright material in this book. Every effort has been made to trace and contact copyright holders. If there are any inadvertent omissions we apologize to those concerned and undertake to include suitable acknowledgements in all future editions.

The Anglican Church in Aotearoa, New Zealand and Polynesia: for extracts taken/adapted from *A New Zealand Prayer Book - He Karikia Mihinare O Aotearoa.*

Cambridge University Press: extracts (and adapted extracts) from *The Book of Common Prayer*, the rights in which are vested in the Crown, are reproduced by permission of the Crown's Patentee, Cambridge University Press.

The Continuum International Publishing Group Ltd: for extracts from Stephen Oliver, *Pastoral Prayers*, Mowbray, 1996 © Mowbray, an imprint of The Continuum International Publishing Group Ltd. Used by permission.

Episcopal Church of the USA: for extracts from *The Book of Common Prayer* according to the use of the Episcopal Church of the USA, 1979. The ECUSA Prayer Book is not subject to copyright.

Grove Books: for extracts from Trevor Lloyd, *Liturgy and Death*, Grove Books © Trevor Lloyd.

Intellectual Properties Management, Atlanta, Georgia: for 'And now to him who is able . . .' by Martin Luther King. License granted by Intellectual Properties Management as Exclusive Licensor of the King Estate.

International Committee on English in the Liturgy (ICEL): for English translations based on (or excerpted from *The Roman Missal* © 1973 International Committee on English in the Liturgy (ICEL); also material based (or excerpted from) *The Order of Christian Funerals* © 1985, ICEL. All rights reserved.

Methodist Publishing House: for extract from *The Methodist Worship Book* ©1999 Trustees for Methodist Church Purposes. Used by permission of Methodist Publishing House.

The Saint Andrew Press, Edinburgh: for extracts from *Common Order* © The Church of Scotland Panel on Worship.

SCM Press: for extracts from John A. T. Robinson, 'Learning from Cancer', *Where Three Ways Meet*, SCM Press, 1987.

SPCK: for 'O God who brought us to birth' from Janet Morley, *All Desires Known*, SPCK, 1992 © Janet Morley and for extract from Martin Dudley, *A Manual for Ministry to the Sick*, SPCK, 1997. Used by permission of the publisher.

Preface

Through its Funeral ministry, the Church of England daily touches the lives of very many people. Death is a reality that everyone has to face, both for themselves and for those close to them. People come to terms with death in different ways, but nearly always with pain and difficulty. Practical support for the dying and the bereaved is seen as important, and is looked for from both family and friends. Spiritual support is also seen as important, not least when questions are asked about why 'God' should 'choose' a particular moment in time to 'end' the earthly life of a particular individual. As Anglican ministers have the peculiar privilege of being called to conduct most of the funerals in this country, to them falls the lot of providing such spiritual support, together with some 'answers' to all these ultimate questions. It is not an easy calling; clergy need not only spiritual courage and insight in order to respond adequately, but also good liturgical texts and resources to give prayerful and practical context to their response.

For four hundred years, *The Book of Common Prayer* has been the sole liturgical resource for Anglicans. Together with its twentieth-century revisions, such as the *Burial Services* (Alternative Services Series 1), *The Book of Common Prayer* has given and continues to give theological meaning and spiritual comfort to many facing death and bereavement. More recently, *The Alternative Service Book 1980* provided additional and welcome contemporary liturgical services for those who found the seventeenth-century language and imagery of the Prayer Book unhelpful. Twenty years of using these alternative forms have revealed their weaknesses as well as their strengths. The new *Common Worship* services, created in the light of these and other insights and experiences, give us stronger and more appropriate texts for today, as well as a wider range of helpful worship resources to support our ministry at the time of death.

This guide to the *Common Worship* funeral services is intended to be very practical. It attempts to indicate how Church of England ministers might make best use of these new liturgical resources in today's demanding context for funeral ministry. These suggestions are humbly offered in the light of reflection on two years' experience of using the services in their draft forms in one of the experimental parishes. While they inevitably suffer the constraints of being one person's thoughts, they have been much influenced and shaped by the comments of colleagues from other ministerial situations and ecclesial backgrounds.

R Anne Horton

Introduction
Trevor Lloyd

One of the many recurring themes in both current liturgical and pastoral thinking is that of the journey. The pattern of this introduction is that of a journey through three questions to ask about every journey, every pilgrimage, every progression we make from one stage of life to another.

We are all on a journey through life. Where is God in relation to that journey? He is both the starting point and the ending point, the Alpha and the Omega. Not only that, but as the Psalmist says, in all our rushing around between the beginning and the end, God is there too.

> Where can I go then from your Spirit?
> Or where can I flee from your presence?
> If I climb up to heaven, you are there;
> If I make the grave my bed, you are there also.
> (Psalm 139.7)

An accompanied journey, with questions

So our journey is an accompanied one. God is with us every step of the way. Sometimes the realization of that presence is conveyed to us through the presence of God's people on the journey. As on a medieval pilgrimage, different people on the road have different backgrounds, a variety of family relationships, engage in different occupations and have varied functions in relation to others on the journey. Not all travel at the same speed. Some spend their time specifically helping others along and ministering to them; some imagine their burdens are too great for them to have the ability to help others.

The Funeral service comes towards the end of this journey, and is embedded in a series of rites which may be used sometimes, but not always.

As with other accompanied journeys, there are questions to ask.

- Where are we going and why? (i.e. What is the purpose of this particular journey?)

- Is the company congenial? Are they relatives or friends or new acquaintances?

- Is the journey broken into stages? What are the recognized stopping-off points?

Each of these questions has a theological motivation.

Where are we going and why?

'Where are we going and why?' is one of the ultimate questions, related to the purpose and meaning of the universe. Any individual journey from life to death is a contribution to the answer to the question. One answer might be 'from earth to heaven'. So there is a place for emphasizing both the earthiness of the starting point and the heavenliness of the destination. Whether the starting point is the deathbed in a hospital or at home, where someone may be dying in pain or unconscious, or whether it is a group of grieving and bewildered relations some time later, the awfulness and gravity of the human predicament cannot be avoided and should not be masked or belittled by platitudinous words. Death comes to us all, and is final as far as this life is concerned. 'It is appointed for mortals to die once, and after that the judgement' (Hebrews 9.27).

Celebration

But if the earthly starting point is awe-full, it can also be celebratory, in two ways. The reason why we do not simply throw this dead body on the rubbish heap but treat it with reverence as we dispose of it, is that it has been the dwelling-place of a God-imaged human being. As well as reverence, there

can be thanksgiving to God for the God-given character and
achievements of this person. In the new services, there is
deliberate encouragement for this to happen, in the provision for
a tribute, or for words to be spoken as symbols of the life and
faith of the dead person are placed near the coffin, and in the
wording of some of the prayers:

> Father in heaven,
> we thank you because you made us in your own image
> and gave us gifts in mind, body and spirit.
> We thank you now for N
> and what *he/she* meant to each of us.
>
> *(Prayer 20, p. 352)*

On the road to heaven

The other way in which our earthly starting point can be
celebratory is encapsulated in the words of *The Book of
Common Prayer*, 'Forasmuch as it hath pleased Almighty God to
deliver this our brother from the miseries of this sinful life . . . '.
Such thanksgiving focuses, like the recurring theme of spirituals,
on the anticipated joys of heaven. This is in some ways the
opposite of thanksgiving for the achievements of this life. Rather
the argument is that if this life has been so bad as to be almost
unbearable, surely God must have something better in store for us.

> This world is not my home,
>   I'm just a-passing through;
> my treasures are laid up
>   somewhere beyond the blue . . .

We find this in the new services, for instance in the prayers:

> Bring all who rest in Christ
> into the fullness of your kingdom
> where sins have been forgiven
> and death is no more.
>
> *(Prayers, p. 265)*

Thus the Prayer of Entrusting and Commending (p. 267) moves
from earth: 'God our creator and redeemer', through the cross:

'by your power Christ conquered death', to heaven: 'and entered into glory', and invites us to do the same, 'Confident of his victory and claiming his promises . . .'. The prayer of committal (p. 269) restores a phrase of hope from the 1662 service: 'who will transform our frail bodies that they may be conformed to his glorious body'.

Structure

The structure of the Funeral service is based on this journey from the earthly to the heavenly. It begins by celebrating the humanity of the dead person before moving, through the readings and sermon, towards thinking about heaven in the prayers of commendation and committal. This answer to the question 'Where are we going?' describes something of the movement of the service, its starting point and destination. But there are other answers to the question which set this activity within a larger context. 'Where are we going?' may be the despairing cry of a relative totally distraught and bewildered by death. What is this death-event all about, and does it contribute at all to my growth or self-understanding as a human being? What is this death for, for me and for others here? One purpose of a Funeral must surely be to help some people at least to articulate the question about the meaning of life for them, and to begin to explore some answers. So the Note on the Sermon says: 'The purpose of the Sermon is to proclaim the gospel in the context of the death of this particular person'. The service must not be so heavily constructed to reinforce bland assurances of comfort that there is no scope for challenge, or an exploration of the deeper questions some people will be addressing.

Problems

For some, the question 'Where are we going?' will be especially difficult. In general terms, how far should the Church's Funeral service go in speaking as plainly about the reality of judgement as about the joys of heaven? The Prayer Book service speaks of 'the bitter pain of eternal death'. In more specific terms, problems may arise when the way the service is taken conveys absolute assurance about the heavenly destination of someone who had no time for God, the faith or Christian company during his or her time on earth. The gospel – expressed in one of the passages of Scripture frequently used at Funeral services – seems clear: 'I am the way, the truth and the life: no one comes to the Father but by me'. But the clear gospel reassurance for those who know themselves to be believers can, at the same time, risk appearing to condemn the deceased, whose faith is unknown. This is why some ministers feel it is right, in order not to embarrass grieving relatives, to tone down anything which might be too clear and to resort to the usual comforting platitudes. The minister will have in mind both the demands of the gospel to speak the truth about life, death and judgement, but also the vulnerability of the mourners in this particular situation and the love that Christ has for them in their time of need.

Two kinds of service?

The Liturgical Commission discussed at an early stage whether there should be two kinds of Funeral, one for professing Christians and the other for those who are less certain about what, if anything, they believe. The arguments advanced in favour of this way forward were:

a) that a service which speaks clearly of Christian hope, when there is – as all present may be aware – no evidence of faith, may mislead people into assuming that there really is no need for such Christian faith;

b) that the task of having to devise a Funeral service which can be used without offence by those of little or no faith means that the service cannot speak with sufficient joy and assurance when everyone present has no doubt about the heavenly destination of the departed;

c) that it is biblical to think in terms of two categories: Jesus frequently speaks of such division of people into two classes by their eternal destiny;

d) that some of those present at a Funeral find clear and strong language about the Christian faith hard to take, both for themselves and in relation to the departed person.

The Commission came to the conclusion, supported by the House of Bishops, that there should be one service. The time for the judgement of which Jesus speaks is not yet, nor is that judgement – fortunately – our responsibility: it belongs solely to God. Jesus himself speaks of the foolishness of attempting to root out the weeds from among the wheat: 'Let both of them grow together until the harvest; and at harvest time I will tell the reapers . . .'. There is a long Anglican tradition of making charitable assumptions about people, and questions, on the one hand, about giving offence and, on the other, about a lack of gospel clarity are really questions about pastoral sensitivity, careful preparation and the in-service training of those who minister to the bereaved. So the Commission, far from producing a compromise service, came to the conclusion that a group of Christian liturgists had no mandate or experience to produce a non-Christian service, and that it should be possible to have the same basic rite for all, and not one service for Church members and one for others.

They emphasized this approach by taking as the basic structure, for the first time since the Reformation in the Church of England, not the Office but the Eucharist. To have a fully eucharistic service would clearly be beneficial because:

- The Eucharist is the characteristic Christian thing for Christian families to do, a familiar way for them to pray at a time of stress.

- It ensures the focus is on Christ and not on the corpse.

- It involves using familiar texts.

- It provides a context in which confession and absolution are there not because there are good psychological reasons for them, but because they are part of the rite.

- It emphasizes the nature of the Church as a community which is providing support for the bereaved.

- It ensures that the action, on one level, is set in eternity.

Now, because the Commission never had any assumption that most Funerals would be eucharistic, we might ask how many of these effects are true when it is really the first half of the Eucharist – the word and prayers – which is used as the basis for the structure of the funeral service. Clearly, the familiarity of a recognizable familiar pattern is there for those who are used to the Eucharist, and that will have an effect on some. Both the possibility of penitence and the movement from earth to heaven reflect the Eucharist. The effect of putting the Crucifixion at the centre, rather than the coffin, affected the way in which the rite was planned. Some of the eucharistic feel was toned down a little by the Synod Revision Committee, for example by changing 'Liturgy of the Word' to the more accessible 'Bible Reading and Sermon', but the basic structure is still there, as is the fully worked out Funeral Service within a Celebration of Holy Communion.

Is the company congenial?

The second major question about the Funeral journey was 'Is the company congenial?' Whether there is a large black limousine following the hearse, or the people offer one another lifts from home to church or from the church to the crematorium, these journeys are often marked by awkward silences. This may reflect the fact that this is not a normal journey, it may be caused by embarrassment at not knowing what to say or how to behave, or may conceal a variety of unspoken thoughts. Banal comments about the flowers or the speed of the car may hide deep unspoken longings and questions about the whole meaning of life and the universe. Two important things to grasp about the company on the funeral journey are that it is varied, and that it changes.

Gathering the community

The introduction for reading before the Funeral Service (p. 256) speaks of the varied nature of the congregation – 'We will each have had our own experiences of their life and death, with different memories and different feelings of love, grief and respect' – and speaks of the importance of acknowledging this at the beginning of the service. The Commission originally had several different introductions for different circumstances and groups of people, but amalgamated them for the sake of simplicity. In the Resources for the Funeral of a Child there are two different sets of words for introducing the service, and the selection of prayers includes alternative prayers at the gathering.

The title of the opening section, 'The Gathering', is an indication, not only that these people come together from a variety not only of places but different relationships with the dead person, but also that the task of the minister at the beginning of the service, reflected in the introduction and the gathering prayer, is to attempt to mould this disparate group of people into one congregation. The theological point at issue here is whether it is possible to say of this group of people, 'we are the body of Christ', or whether it is simply a group of spectators watching the minister perform a rite in relation to a dead body. Clearly there will be occasions, for example, when someone dies in a nursing home and the Funeral is attended only by two representatives of the home who have no relationship with the church or with Jesus Christ. At the other end of the scale, those Funerals at which there is a Eucharist clearly imply that at least by the time of the Peace there would have been a welding together of the congregation into some kind of relationship of mutual support and belonging, united respect and love for the dead person, and corporate openness to receiving the Word of God and the Bread of Life. The latent eucharistic structure of the rite, even when there is no Holy Communion, constitutes a slight pressure in this direction, reinforced by such things as the provision, in the Prayers of Penitence, of some element of getting straight with God towards the beginning of the service.

But the underlying – and nagging – theological question remains. Is it possible for this disparate group of people to be so transformed that they can with integrity say, 'We are the body of Christ'? How can those gathered exhibit the characteristics of a true eucharistic community? To ask this question is to raise the question of the relationship of the Funeral community to the local Christian community: it is clearly more possible to behave eucharistically when the dead person is part of the local Christian assembly, and many of them are present. It is much more difficult when the only representatives of that community are the vicar and the verger. Perhaps, on the analogy of encouraging members of the church to be present at a baptism which is not part of a main service, church councils should consider whether it might be right to encourage church members to be present at Funerals where most of the congregation might otherwise be visitors.

A mobile community

On many journeys the company changes as you go along. This is obviously true of a train or bus with stations or stops at which people get on or off, but it is also true of a walking group, say on a pilgrimage. As the walk goes on, you meet up with different people and converse with them. This is true of the process of dying and bereavement, and is reflected in the services provided. At times the company may be small and intimate, the immediate family or close friends, for instance, by the bedside of a dying person, or a slightly wider group welcoming the coffin into church the day before the Funeral. At other times, for instance the main Funeral service or a memorial service, the company may be composed of a variety of groups each having a different relationship to the dead person.

Is the journey broken into stages? What are the recognized stopping-off points?

The third major question about the accompanied journey is: 'Is the journey broken into stages? What are the recognized stopping-off points?' Grief is not a once-for-all event, any more than a death invariably occurs all at once. Grieving is a process which may begin before death if a person is terminally ill or unconscious.

The period from the moment of death to coming home after the Funeral may seem like a roller-coaster of emotions, with an element of numbness and getting through the many practical things there are to do, almost on auto-pilot. Sometimes the process protects people from facing the truth that this person has died, and the truth does not begin to sink in until after the

Funeral. Any pastoral theology needs to recognize both that this turmoil exists in different ways in different bereaved families, and that it is a crucial part of a much longer process of grieving. It is helpful to look for 'stopping-off' points where the family can draw breath and be helped to put a little of their turmoil of emotions into context, so that they might be more easily accepted and integrated at a later stage. Connections between God and the bereaved people can be made at different points before the Funeral, sometimes giving greater depth to the service itself.

History and movement

The current – and pastorally less than helpful – focusing of the Funeral into one short service is something we have had with us since the time of the Reformation. The 1964 Report of the Liturgical Commission on The Burial of the Dead started from the Reformation and the debates at that time. So it saw 'the chief theological question involved' as prayer for the dead. The current work of the Liturgical Commission both starts much further back and is also wider in its theology, putting prayer about the departed into this wider context. The basic structure of the underlying series of events, which used to have a liturgical accompaniment, is determined by the need to move: from the place of dying to the place of worship, to the place of burial. The pattern of the Roman secular funeral, early Roman Christian rites (for example in the Rheinau Sacramentary of 800) and of thirteenth-century and later monastic liturgy, sees the Funeral rite as a continuum, broken by movements from place to place, from home to church, to the place of burial and back to the home.

It was this pattern which was severely truncated by the actions of the Reformers. The problems associated with the medieval doctrine of purgatory and the corrupt practices associated with prayer for the dead led the Reformers to throw out the baby with the bath water, and to exclude any liturgical prayer before or after the service at the graveside from the 1552 Prayer Book. What the Commission has done, with wide approval both from the eight hundred parishes which trialled these services, and from the General Synod, where no one voted against the final approval of the Funeral Service, is to open the door to looking again at Funerals as a continuum of rites, a series of prayers and services. This should prove to be pastorally helpful, and has been done in a way which – as far as the official text is concerned – avoids the old doctrinal problems.

'Staged rites'

'Staged rites' is the term which has come to be used not for the staging or performance of a rite but for the breaking up of the rite into a number of different stages. One way of thinking about this is to use the Latin word *limen* which means 'threshold'. This is the word from which we get our English word 'preliminary', meaning that which happens before a crucial event. The actual crisis, the centre of the event, may then be labelled '*liminal*', and that which happens afterwards '*post-liminal*'. So with a Funeral there are a number of *pre-liminary* rites, from ministry at the time of death in its various forms, through the prayers to be used at home before the Funeral, and on the morning of the Funeral, and the receiving of the body into church, together with the possibility of a Funeral vigil. And after the Funeral, the *post-liminal* rites include some prayers said on returning home, memorial prayers and services and possibly the burial of ashes.

Catching-up time

Part of this approach involves seeing the central event, the crisis, as the moment of disintegration, the moment prepared for in the preliminaries, when something totally new happens; a new and possibly unknown state is entered into. This needs to be followed by elements of re-integration, as the event is reflected upon and absorbed into the ongoing life. One of the difficulties here is that when you ask about the nature of the central event in the Funeral, that event must surely be the death, which in this scenario occurs at some point during the Ministry at the Time of Death. This gives to the Funeral service and all that follows the task of re-integration, absorbing the crisis event into the ongoing life. But from the liturgical point of view, it is the Funeral service itself which has to bear the weight of being the crisis moment.

This way of thinking, as well as providing a helpful rationale for the different stages of the total collection of rites, has one important effect on the Funeral service itself. In the diverse groups assembled as mourners, there will be very few who have been at the bedside or wherever the death has taken place. The early part of the Funeral service therefore needs to act as a catching-up time, a recapitulation of the event that has taken place, and of the thoughts and feelings of those present. One simple way in which this can be seen is that the Funeral service can start with the reception of the body into the church, which could equally well have happened the day before, with a smaller number of people present. One of the effects of this recapitulation is that there are some kinds of Prayers of Commendation and prayers for the well-being of the departed in heaven, which may be perfectly acceptable for everyone to pray as the person approaches death, or even as they are dying, but which would be unacceptable to some people to pray at a later stage. However, if the early part of the Funeral service is seen as a recapitulation of the moments of dying, it may be more acceptable to pray in this way at that point in this service, as all present are brought into a realization of that moment when heaven meets earth and the mystery of death is being explored.

The main themes

Each of the stages on the journey has its own bundle of theological issues, while all share in reflecting the underlying themes of the Funeral service: the certainty and finality of death, the nature of the Church and the community of saints, the certainty of the resurrection and the love, comfort and strength of God conveyed through his Holy Spirit.

Ministry at the Time of Death

In Ministry at the Time of Death, as well as these themes, there is a preliminary focus at the beginning on repentance and forgiveness. This can be as brief or as elaborate as the dying person and the minister wish to make it. But it is a useful reminder, which may be used by those teaching about preparing for dying and death, of the need for each of us to be in a state of forgiveness all the time. It also provides an important opportunity for a personal ministry of reconciliation. The service then moves into a mode where the doors of heaven are open, and there is an interplay between heaven and earth as the sights of all present are set on the future hope.

Prayer when someone has just died continues this theme, marking and reinforcing the fact of death:

> The old order has passed away.

Prayer at Home before the Funeral

Prayer at Home before the Funeral speaks largely of the love of God: the words 'comfort' and 'consolation' recur. But there is another bit of theology at work here, a more subtle sacramental activity. What is the pre-Funeral visit for? It may look as if it is just to bring a little comfort to the bereaved, and to sort out the all-important details about the Funeral service. But in encouraging the bereaved to rehearse both the immediate story of how the death happened, and the longer story of the person's life, the minister is not only engaging in a useful therapy as the bereaved come to terms with what has happened, but also making the important connections between these people, these feelings, this celebration of life or need for forgiveness and comfort, and God. God is present and interested in all of this. For some, the presence of the minister will symbolize that interest of God himself.

Receiving the Coffin at Church before the Funeral

Similarly, receiving the coffin at church the day before the Funeral symbolizes a 'coming home to rest' for those who have been used to being with God's people in church, being at home with the rest of the body of Christ, and should provide space and time for reflection, which is taken up and amplified if there is a vigil. Prayer on the morning of the Funeral fills that empty, waiting space, the uncertainty before crossing over yet another threshold, with the presence of God, a kind of holding God's hand as we go forward into the day of the Funeral.

Prayer at Home after the Funeral

Afterwards, the prayers at home after the Funeral provide an opportunity for recognizing God's presence in the home, focusing on the table and recognizing Jesus in the breaking of bread, like the two on the road to Emmaus after the resurrection. This picks up on the practicalities of having food on the table for which this can be the grace, and using that to provide a forward, Christ-centred look at what the future holds:

> Almighty God, the Father of our Lord Jesus Christ,
> whose disciples recognized him as he broke bread
>   at their table after the resurrection:
> we thank you for your strength upholding us
>   in what we have done today,
> and now we ask for your presence to be recognized in
>   this home . . .
>
> *(Prayers, p. 321)*

The Burial of Ashes

The Burial of Ashes deals with the practicality of burying ashes, but uses the nature of the substance itself as a link with Psalm 90 ('You turn us back to dust' – one of the sentences for use at the beginning of the service), and thus as a reminder of the brevity of life:

> As we remember N in this place,
> hold before us our beginning and our ending,
> the dust from which we come
> and the death to which we move . . .
>
> *(Prayers, p. 330)*

So all through our journey we discover and rediscover this interplay of theology and action, practical things to be done alongside theological questions to ask, an interplay in which the text and substance of the services have their part, and which leads us forward in our own spiritual journey.

PART I
Context

I The Church's ministry at the time of death

Death, faith and worship

From the earliest days, Christians have joined together to worship God at moments of significant change in their lives. The most significant changes in all our lives are undeniably birth and death, the beginning and ending of life. Christian acts of worship at these major 'life and death' moments are commonly known as 'pastoral' or 'occasional' services. In them, we worship God in the context, for example, of birth, of marriage, of illness and of death.

The Church of England recognizes two gospel sacraments, Baptism and Eucharist. The Funeral Service, while not a sacrament, does contain some sacramental characteristics. Symbols and symbolic acts are an important part of the worship. The symbolic acts within the service represent and celebrate God's gracious presence and activity at every moment of our lives, and so help us to grow as spiritual people as we adjust to and find meaning in all life's changes.

A major requirement of Christian ministry at the time of death is that it should help people make spiritual and theological sense of physical death at whatever stage in life it occurs. In its pastoral ministry, the Church supports and cares for its members as they prepare for, cope with and come to terms with the reality of dying, death and bereavement. In its liturgical ministry, through words and symbolic actions, the Church's worship ministers God's healing grace to his people, enabling them to affirm and be affirmed by their resurrection faith despite their deep feelings of inadequacy and pain in the face of death.

Death is the ultimate and inescapable 'life transition'. It is a condition of the life of Christians just as much as it is of the life of non-Christians. St Augustine once preached:

> As when medical men examine an illness and ascertain that it is fatal, they make this pronouncement, 'He will die, he will not get over this,' so from the moment of a man's birth, it may be said, 'He will not get over this.'
>
> *Sermon 47, 3*

Christianity is earthed in this realism about the inevitability of death. It does not seek to evade the reality of death, nor to offer a way of escape, nor some psychological technique for minimizing the trauma of grief. Rather, Christian faith sets the supernatural realism of eternal life alongside the natural realism of physical death. Because Christians believe in a God who created them, loves them, and sustains them, from birth, through life and death, to all eternity, they can face death, however reluctantly, with spiritual confidence. Physical death is not the end of everything. It is change, it is 'new start', new opportunity.

The Church's liturgy, through its pastoral and Funeral services, gives a faith context to death, whether it be sudden or as a result of illness. The various church services and prayers bring to those who worship through them an increasing understanding of how, as Christians, they might think, feel, act and grow through these particular life crises. In worship, all our emotions surrounding death – grief, shock, anger, disbelief, doubt, and so on – are brought face to face with Almighty God, and are, in his grace and mercy, and in time, transformed. The ultimate theological test of Funeral services and prayers, therefore, is whether they have the power to enable all of this, in the many and varied circumstances in which they are used.

Each death is unique and different. While, for example, grief is a primary emotion in most bereavements, it does not always dominate: so the Funeral of a Christian who dies peacefully and full of years can reflect thanksgiving and rejoicing for a soul who has 'gone to glory'. In another situation, death may come after months and years of pain and distress, and then a Funeral might rightly reflect the natural feelings of relief that the pain and distress are now things of the past. On the other hand, many deaths are experienced as untimely and unfair, and the Funeral service needs to acknowledge and respond to people's feelings of disbelief, outrage and shock. The pastoral challenge to the Church's liturgists is to produce a set of services that are strong enough and flexible enough to respond to the demands of every set of circumstances.

Making theological sense of death

'Do you think heaven is an eternal party?' A regular communicant who was dying asked this question of one of her clergy. Having been told this by another Christian, she was wrestling with the concept, and indeed with her Christian faith. Another church-goer whose dying husband was an atheist was tormented by the worry that this meant that she and he would ultimately be on opposite sides of the final great divide. A Betterware salesman on a rectory doorstep asked the rector how Christians thought they could get to heaven: was it all down to Jesus, or did life-style make a difference? And the perennial question was asked by a young adult whose brother, a relatively new Christian, had just committed suicide: how can you believe in an almighty and loving God who 'allows' my brother to take his own life? God isn't 'fair'. Christians, like everyone else, wrestle with all these questions and many more.

Most of the time, people's reactions and feelings about death are kept very much under wraps. The sudden death of a prominent public figure like the Princess of Wales some years ago revealed quite a lot about 'popular' reactions to and beliefs about death. Many people watched her Funeral service at Westminster Abbey. How effective was that service in helping those who watched it to make Christian sense of a death that had affected so many of them so deeply?

Clergy and ministers have the responsibility of preparing people for death, conducting their Funerals and supporting them through bereavement. Our services are vital instruments for fulfilling these responsibilities. The prayers, readings and music chosen, the sermons preached, the way the worship is conducted, all these have teaching as well as pastoral potential.

For many people, the Funeral service may be their only exposure to the expression of Christian worship and belief. But how good is the Funeral service at helping people make sense of death and Christian faith? And should the Funeral service be the only liturgical opportunity for Christians to learn how to approach death? No one goes to that many Funerals in their lifetime. How good are the regular Sunday services of the Church at helping people grow in their theological understanding of these ultimate questions, perhaps through the patterns of reading Scripture, the credal affirmations and the prayers? And what about the way we use other liturgical opportunities through the Church Year, such as Holy Week, Good Friday, All Souls' Day and Remembrance Sunday?

To some extent questions about a theological understanding of death will raise issues of churchmanship and variations of doctrinal understanding, more particularly perhaps for clergy and ministers. Great care has been taken in the evolution of these services and prayers to respect doctrinal differences, yet to provide a liturgy to which all can say 'Amen', even if they might want to make certain choices rather than other ones.

The first impression given by the *Common Worship* Funeral services and the related pastoral material is that, in contrast with both *The Alternative Service Book* and *The Book of Common Prayer*, there are so many different texts. The comparative tables below (Ministry at the Time of Death; Before and After the Funeral; Funeral Services) contrast the provision made in *Common Worship* with earlier books. A further look at the details of the provision also indicates a distinct move in emphasis. No longer are we concerned solely with the reverent disposal of a body in the context of Christian faith and worship, important though that is. We are now also honouring the life and relationships of the dead person and the pastoral care of living people – sick people, dying people, bereaved people.

Funeral provision in the Church of England: Comparative tables

Ministry at the Time of Death

Common Worship	Authorized Alternative Rites (1983)	Series 1	The Book of Common Prayer
Preparation, Reconciliation Word of God, Prayers Laying on of Hands with Prayer, and Anointing Holy Communion Commendation	Prayers for Use with the Sick Laying on of Hands with Prayer, and Anointing Communion with the Sick A Commendation at the Time of Death		Order for the Visitation of the Sick The Communion of the Sick
Prayer when someone has just died			

Before and After the Funeral

Common Worship	The Alternative Service Book	Series 1	The Book of Common Prayer
At Home before the Funeral For those Unable to be Present at the Funeral Receiving the Coffin at Church before the Funeral A Funeral Vigil On the Morning of the Funeral	A Service which may be used before a Funeral		
At Home after the Funeral			
The Burial of Ashes	A Form which may be used at the Interment of the Ashes		
Memorial Service			
Resources: Prayers, Readings, Canticles	A Selection of Additional Prayers which may be used		

Funeral Services

Common Worship	The Alternative Service Book	Series 1	The Book of Common Prayer
Outline Order for Funerals The Funeral Service The Funeral Service within a Celebration of Holy Communion Outline Order for the Funeral of a Child Outline Order for the Funeral of a Child within a Celebration of Holy Communion	Funeral Service The Funeral Service with Holy Communion The Funeral of a Child	An Order for the Burial of the Dead An Order for the Burial of a Child	The Order for the Burial of the Dead
Resources for the Funeral of a Child	Prayers after the Birth of a still-born Child or the Death of a newly-born Child		

What does the *Common Worship* Funeral Service say about death?

The Opening Sentences:

> 'Those who believe in me, even though they die, will live, and everyone who lives and believes in me will never die.'
>
> *John 11.25, 26 (p. 259)*

Gathering Prayers:

> God of all consolation,
> your Son Jesus Christ was moved to tears
> at the grave of Lazarus his friend.
>
> *(p. 260)*

> Almighty God,
> you judge us with infinite mercy and justice,
> and love everything you have made.
>
> *(p. 260)*

The Collect:

> . . . all who have died in the love of Christ
> will share in his resurrection.
>
> *(p. 262)*

The Committal:

> ...in sure and certain hope of the resurrection to eternal life
> through our Lord Jesus Christ,
> who will transform our frail bodies
> that they may be conformed to his glorious body.
>
> *(p. 269)*

> We look for the fullness of the resurrection
> when Christ shall gather all his saints
> to reign with him in glory for ever.
>
> *(p. 269)*

Preparation of the Table:

> May all who are called to a place at your table
> follow in the way that leads to the unending feast of life.
>
> *(p. 283)*

The Eucharistic Prayer (Preface):

> ...although death comes to us all,
> yet we rejoice in the promise of eternal life;
> for to your faithful people life is changed, not taken away;
> and when our mortal flesh is laid aside
> an everlasting dwelling place is made ready for us in heaven.
>
> *(p. 283)*

Prayer after Communion:

> Gracious God,
> grant that this sacrament may be to us
> ...a pledge of our inheritance
> in that kingdom where there is no death
> ...but fullness of joy with all your saints.
>
> *(p. 286)*

Blessing:

> God the Father,
> ...open to you who believe the gates of everlasting life.
> **Amen.**
>
> *(p. 290)*

The *Common Worship* Funeral and related pastoral services have been carefully constructed to express the core doctrinal beliefs of the Church of England. Whatever their doctrinal position, clergy and ministers will want to ask how they can so plan and preside over the services in order that they might best fulfil this educational role. The better we are able to help people grow in their understanding of the place of death for Christians, the fewer pastoral problems we should experience when death finally has to be faced.

Working with the grief process

Grief is a normal response to death, both in anticipation and when it happens. Today we are more aware than we used to be of the grieving process that characterizes bereavement. The contents and wording of the *Common Worship* Funeral and pastoral material reflect this awareness. For the services to achieve their full potential, those who preside over them must be aware of, and sensitive to, both the stages of grief in the people to whom they minister, and also the way in which the various prayers and readings might minister to each particular stage. It is important to know how the various stages of grief are reflected in the Funeral and pastoral rites. (In the following section, the numbers refer to the 'Prayers for Use with the Dying and at Funeral and Memorial Services' in the Resources section.)

How do the *Common Worship* services address the grief process?

Shock and disbelief – our model of the world is upset; we not only lose a person close to us but life also can feel as if it has lost its meaning. Shock can take the form of numbness or physical pain, complete apathy, withdrawal, abnormal calm and, in some cases, anger.

Common Worship

- encourages people to remain with the dying person until death occurs, and to pray with them and for them. The notes relating to 'Ministry at the Time of Death' explicitly mention the presence of 'family and friends'.

- acknowledges feelings of shock, denial, confusion and anger in the prayers for those who mourn. 'O God, who brought us to birth, and in whose arms we die, in our grief and shock contain and comfort us' (p. 354); 'Do not let grief overwhelm your children, or turn them against you' (p. 355); 'Let us find in your Son comfort in our sadness, certainty in our doubt, and courage to live' (p. 357); 'Merciful God, . . . you know the anguish of our hearts. It is beyond our understanding and more than we can bear' (p. 359).

Denial – usually felt during the first fourteen days. We can behave as if the death has not happened and the dead person is still there, e.g. routine activities, making plans.

Common Worship

- encourages us to talk about the person who has died. In some of the services and prayers 'Before the Funeral', the bereaved may share memories of the departed in the context of the Bible readings and prayers.

- speaks aloud the reality of the death through the wording of the prayers. Many of the prayers are particular and not general: 'Lord we come into your presence to remember N.' The prayers help mourners acknowledge the death and their emotional reactions to it.

- offers additional liturgical resources for the time between the death and the Funeral. Prayers are given to be said at home, or on hearing of a death, or at a vigil in church or at home.

- pays more direct attention to the coffin, encouraging people to come near it and to name the dead body within it. At the reception of the coffin, 'we receive the body of our *brother/sister* N' (p. 242), family, friends or other members of the congregation may place suitable symbols of the life and faith of the departed person on or near the coffin.

25

Growing awareness – acknowledgement of the reality of the death often comes in waves of savage and uncontrollable feelings, such as tears, anger, guilt, sadness and loneliness. We need to 'go over' the death, trying to find a reason for it, or we revisit the place where it happened. We often feel angry – at the deceased, the medical services, friends and family, or God – for letting it happen. There are feelings of despair, emptiness, pain of loss, together with feelings of not being needed, or of there being no point to our own life. Sometimes we feel guilty: 'if only I had done this or that, or if only I had loved him/her more . . .'. We also experience panic and anxiety attacks, as we realize the extent of our loss and the demands of our future without the deceased.

Common Worship

- acknowledges that grief is normal. A prayer at the beginning of the Funeral service reminds us that even Jesus was moved to tears at the grave of his friend Lazarus.

- encourages the sharing of memories of the departed especially during the time before the Funeral. There is provision for prayers at home, or in church, before the Funeral.

- encourages the honouring of the life of the departed in the Funeral and memorial services. The 'Notes to the Funeral Service' allow for a tribute or tributes to be made, 'remembering and honouring the life of the person who has died, and the evidence of God's grace and work in them' (p. 291).

- allows us to pray for ourselves and for our own needs. The prayers include, for example: 'Lift us from anxiety and guilt' (p. 348); 'Heal our memories of hurt and failure' (p. 354) 'We are angry at the loss we have sustained' (p. 355).

- by mentioning tears in the prayers, gives us permission to cry. 'We cry to you, O Lord, you gave *him/her* to us and you have taken *him/her* away' (p. 358); 'Be with

them [the mourners] as they weep' (p. 356); 'Help us,
through our tears and pain' (p. 358).

- addresses, in some of the prayers, feelings of
  loneliness, isolation, despair, darkness, anxiety, guilt
  and anger. 'Out of the depths I cry to you' (p. 349);
  'Spare them the torment of guilt and despair' (p. 356);
  'Draw near to us as we walk this lonely road' (p. 357);
  'Give your strength and presence in those daily tasks
  which used to be shared' (p. 321).

- offers worship and prayers for critical moments, e.g.
  in the time in between death and Funeral; returning
  home after the death or Funeral.

- includes prayers of penitence. In the Funeral Service:
  'God of mercy, . . . We turn from the wrong that we have
  thought and said and done, and are mindful of all
  that we have failed to do . . . forgive us' (p. 261).

- involves us in additional symbolic actions around the
  coffin that affirm both the faith of the deceased and
  our own faith. When placing a Bible on the coffin:
  'Your eternal promises to us and to N are proclaimed
  in the Bible'. Or a cross: 'for love of N and each
  one of us you bore our sins on the cross' (p. 244).

Acceptance – occurs much later, usually in the second year,
after the reliving of the death at the first anniversary. As
acceptance grows, we are increasingly able to relearn the
world and new situations with their possibilities and
changes without the deceased person.

Common Worship

- stresses the importance of annual memorial or
  anniversary services and prayers, and mentions the
  provision for annual memorial services in *The
  Promise of his Glory* the forthcoming *Common Worship*
  Times and Seasons volume.

- helps us see the Holy Communion service as the
  activity of the whole church, in paradise and on earth.

At the Preparation of the Table: 'May all who are called to a place at your table follow in the way that leads to the unending feast of life' (p. 283). A preface for use in the Eucharistic Prayer: 'we join with angels and archangels, with [N *and*] all your faithful people' (p. 284).

- offers optional prayers that can be used later on in remembrance of and thanksgiving for the faithful departed. Some of the prayers of thanksgiving, for example, could be used (or adapted for use) at different stages of grieving, and not just at the time of the Funeral.

- encourages us to prepare for our own death by providing 'Prayers for Readiness to live in the Light of Eternity'.

Death: Church and community

Death is never a private thing, though we are often tempted to treat it as such, especially when those who have died are not members of any faith community. The Church of England's Funeral services have to provide for both the spiritual and emotional needs of those who are not practising members of the Church as much as for those who are. Does the Funeral material in *Common Worship* serve the needs of both communities?

All Funerals focus around the particular person who has died, and a death always creates communities of grief. To that extent, the increased emphases in the new services on personalizing each Funeral and on responding to people's emotional as well as spiritual needs at the time of death should be more effective in expressing God's love to those on the fringes of, or outside, the church community.

When members of a church community die, there is more likelihood that other members of the church will be involved, both as bereaved and grieving themselves, and as a supportive community for the family and friends of the deceased.

John died suddenly and unexpectedly in his fifties. He was a prominent member of the church and the local community. As a Reader in the Church, he had been involved in taking Funerals and offering bereavement support himself. He lunched regularly at the local pub and was involved in many of the activities of the village as well as of the church. His work involved him in a variety of wider community networks, where he had made many friends. His sudden death resulted in grief for several communities of people, as well as amongst his family and friends.

His parish priest and fellow lay ministers in the church grieved the loss of a colleague and a friend. Fellow members of the PCC grieved the loss of someone who had worked hard with them for the life of the church. The congregation mourned a caring lay minister and a friend. The Funeral services and additional rites had to address the needs and expectations of all these people.

The close family's private needs were addressed by a 'private' service of the reception of the coffin the night before the Funeral, an early morning Holy Communion service and a prayer beside the empty grave. Family and close friends, including church and village friends, came to the burial service. Friends and contacts from his wider networks joined his family for a thanksgiving service later on the same day.

All the services and most of the prayers were taken from the *Common Worship* provision. Despite some 'unexpected' symbolic acts, such as placing his Bible and a cross on the coffin, all felt that the services they attended had met their needs and were true to their memories of John.

The pastoral situation described above related to a sudden death for which no one was prepared. In the case of a church member who is known to be dying, *Common Worship* does offer several possibilities that might help the ministry team and church community prepare for and work through the deaths of church members. Some of the resources could well also support family members of the individual concerned. It is important, however, that whatever is done in liturgical and pastoral ministry respects both questions of confidentiality and also the individual's rights and needs for privacy. However much one person's death affects their wider community, that death is also the most intimate of encounters between the individual and God.

With the permission of the individuals, their names might be included in the regular intercessions in church services. The sick person might also invite particular people to join in home Holy Communion services or other prayers. If it does not already do so, the parish might well consider incorporating the Laying on of Hands and Anointing at the Holy Communion service into its regular pattern of worship (cf *Common Worship* services of Wholeness and Healing).

Common Worship

We have many and great expectations of our corporate worship within the life of the Church. People will always ask whether new services about to be introduced are really any better than the old ones. The *Common Worship* Funeral services are required to serve the spiritual and emotional needs of people facing death well into the twenty-first century. Do these services and prayers actually help people today make some spiritual and theological sense of the fact of death, however it comes? Do they assist mourners in coping emotionally with the trauma of loss? Are they accessible for people both inside and outside the community of the church? And do they help living people prepare for their own death however distant that might seem?

The chapters that follow look in greater detail at the *Common Worship* provision for the Church's ministry around death. Part 2 addresses the details of the texts themselves. Part 3 suggests ways in which the new services and prayers might be used. The final chapter suggests some sample printed resources that could be created in the parish to support its Funeral and pastoral ministry.

PART 2
Services and prayers

2 The authorized Funeral Services

A change in emphasis

The Book of Common Prayer

In *Common Worship* we have moved a long way from the world
of *The Book of Common Prayer*. The seventeenth-century parson
had but the three texts with which to minister to his sick and
dead parishioners: there were orders for the Visitation of the
Sick, the Communion of the Sick and the Burial of the Dead.
These were practical rites. The rubrics reflected the pastoral
needs of the day, as well as the theological beliefs. Death came
swiftly and suddenly; the major pastoral requirement was to
equip people to meet their Maker. The proposed 1928 revisions
of *The Book of Common Prayer* were relatively minor, but they
did serve to lessen the almost harsh austerity of the 1662 service.
The first part of the revised rite was now to be conducted inside
the church; additional optional prayers for the departed and for
those who mourn were included. And, for the first time, an order
'which may be used for the burial of a child' was included.

The Burial Services (Alternative Services Series 1), which are
authorized for use until 31 December 2005, were a development
of the 1928 proposals. The services are of *Book of Common
Prayer* style, but re-ordered, so that the major part of the service,
lessons and prayers, can all be conducted inside the church
building (or crematorium) with, normally, interment at the end.
Rubrics and texts provide for the celebration of the Holy
Communion, for a committal when the remains are cremated and
for the burial of ashes after cremation. There is a special
variation of the service for the Burial of a Child. In addition, the
'Service in Church', together with the Prayers, may be used as a
Memorial Service.

The Alternative Service Book 1980

The Funeral provision in *The Alternative Service Book* attempted the additional agenda of communicating a more contemporary theological Christian vision, as well as addressing more specifically the spiritual needs of the sick, the dying and the bereaved. Theologically, there was a much greater emphasis on Christian joy and on the resurrection hope: an aspect of the 1960s 'back to historical basics' approach to liturgy which was evident throughout *The Alternative Service Book*. Practically, provision was made for cremations as well as for burials; the material for the Funerals of children was expanded; and there was increased sensitivity to the pastoral needs of the sick, the dying and the bereaved. This latter trend towards a more pastoral liturgy was extended in 1983, when further 'alternative rites' for ministry to the sick and dying were authorized.

In all of this, the varying emphases in the Church of England with regard to praying for the departed were addressed carefully. Generally, *The Alternative Service Book* put prayer for individuals in the context of the Church's prayers for the future of all the faithful: 'Remember, O Lord, this your servant, who has gone before us. . . According to your promises, grant to *him* and to all who rest in Christ, refreshment, light and peace . . .' (Funeral Prayers).

Common Worship

The *Common Worship* Funeral services and prayers take some of the *1928 Prayer Book* and *Alternative Service Book* trends further, and counter others.

A major criticism of *The Alternative Service Book* Funeral Service was that it over-emphasized resurrection joy at the expense of natural human feelings of grief, confusion and doubt. In addition, *The Alternative Service Book* text seemed to address those within the official Christian fold rather than those on its edge, whereas *The Book of Common Prayer* had been more 'inclusive' in its liturgical reach. *Common Worship* has responded to these criticisms. It is arguably more inclusive than *The Alternative Service Book*. It is also far more sensitive than any of its predecessors in its response to natural human feelings at the time of death, while maintaining appropriate witness to the resurrection hope.

Although the services still 'kick in', as it were, at the point of death, the new provisions allow for a passage of experience and emotions. Liturgical provision is made for every stage of the journey from dying, through death and the immediate days before and after the Funeral, to a memorial service and annual memorials and anniversaries. A new factor is a tentative encouragement of the 'personal touch' in funerals, though that encouragement is hedged about with precautions.

The varied understandings in the Church of England over specific prayer for the departed have been carefully addressed. The prayers in the basic Funeral service are acceptable to all. Those who would wish to make specific prayer for the departed will find that some of the optional prayers for use with those who are dying can be adapted for this alternative context.

One of the strengths of *Common Worship* may prove to be its carefully worded notes. These are both explanatory and advisory, and greatly help the minister preparing to take the service. Those who want to get the most out of the texts should read the notes first, though for pastoral reasons these are printed at the end of the service order.

Authorized and commended texts

The provision of commended as well as authorized texts in the new liturgies is relatively new but extremely helpful. The authorized rites are the approved alternatives to the services in *The Book of Common Prayer*. As such, they carry the full weight of formal synodical authority and are seen to be doctrinally consistent with the Anglican position. The commended texts provide optional additional resources for worship in the parish. Although the House of Bishops has commended these rites and prayers, they have not had to undergo the full synodical authorization treatment.

The *Common Worship* material for Funerals and other occasions before and after death contains both authorized and commended material (see the table opposite). The authorized material includes the Funeral Service and the form for the Burial of Ashes. The commended forms offer a variety of pastorally helpful resources to support parochial ministry at the time of death and afterwards.

Common Worship: authorized and commended Funeral material

Authorized material

The Outline Order for Funerals

The Funeral Service

The Funeral Service within a celebration of
   Holy Communion

Supplementary Texts (excluding Sentences)

The Burial of Ashes

Resources: Collects, Prayers of Entrusting and Commending

Commended material

Ministry at the Time of Death

Before the Funeral

   – At Home before the Funeral

   – For those Unable to be Present at the Funeral

   – Receiving the Coffin at Church before the Funeral

   – A Funeral Vigil

   – On the Morning of the Funeral

The Outline Order for the Funeral of a Child

The Outline Order for the Funeral of a Child within
   a celebration of Holy Communion

Resources for the Funeral of a Child

Supplementary Texts: Sentences

After the Funeral

   – At Home after the Funeral

Outline Orders for a Memorial Service

Resources: Prayers, Bible Readings, Canticles

The authorized material

The Outline Order for Funerals

An outline order for a Funeral service precedes the full Funeral order. An outline order is an authorized framework and should not be confused with the 'structure' of a service. The Outline Order gives permission to construct a Funeral service for circumstances when the straightforward use of the approved service is felt to be inappropriate. The Outline Order not only lists the necessary contents but also, and helpfully, gives an overall feel of the service to be created.

The Order contains six headings: Gathering; Readings and Sermon; Prayers; Commendation and Farewell; Committal; Dismissal. These are necessary parts of the Funeral service. Instructions are also given as to what to do should the Funeral Service take place in the context of a Holy Communion service.

The Gathering: there must be a welcome and introduction.

The Gathering has six elements: reception of the coffin at the door of the church, sentences of Scripture, a welcome and introduction to the service, a tribute, Prayers of Penitence and the Collect. While the reception, sentences, tribute, Prayers of Penitence and Collect 'may be' part of the Gathering, there must be a welcome and introduction.

Readings and Sermon: there must be one Bible reading and a Sermon.

There may be more than one Bible reading, and psalms and hymns may follow the readings.

Prayers: there must be some prayers.

A recommended sequence is given: thanksgiving for the life of the departed; prayer for those who mourn; prayers of penitence (if not already used); prayer for readiness to live in the light of eternity.

Commendation and Farewell

This is an essential part of the service, and authorized words must be used.

The Committal

This is also an essential part of the service and an authorized form of words must be used.

The Dismissal

The service may end with a blessing.

Outline orders, such as this one and the order in 'A Service of the Word' (the framework governing non-eucharistic daily and Sunday worship), are a relatively new aspect of Church of England liturgy. They are far from being simple summaries of the structure of authorized services. Rather, they give ministers the freedom to be pastorally sensitive in the construction of worship, while not losing the common ethos of Anglican liturgy.

The distressing pastoral circumstances around the Funeral of a child, for example, have been sensitively addressed by providing an outline order for a service, together with a collection of resources of words, readings and prayers, all of which have been especially created and gathered for use at the Funeral of a child.

Another situation, all too common, where the provision of an outline order should prove helpful, is the short crematorium slot. In the pastorally difficult circumstances where only some twenty minutes or so is allowed for a service, the outline order focuses the minister's mind on what is absolutely necessary: Welcome and Introduction, Bible reading, Sermon, Prayers, Commendation, Committal and Dismissal.

The Funeral Service

Pastoral Introduction

The order of the Funeral service is preceded by a text that can be included within a printed order of service so that the congregation can read it before the service begins.

Structure

A summary structure of the service is printed before the full text. The structure, not to be confused with the 'outline order', makes clear what are the essential elements of the Funeral service. Those parts of the service that are seen as good and helpful but not essential are bracketed.

A quick but informed look at the structure reveals one recurring feature that it is hoped will help make Church of England worship more nearly 'common' worship. The structure of the basic Funeral service looks very similar to the structure of the Holy Communion service – but without any 'Liturgy of the Sacrament'. This will be the normal structure for the majority of the *Common Worship* services. The words used to define the structure are intended to emphasize the commonality of worship, not to suggest that the eucharistic structure is normative. The title of 'Reading(s) and Sermon', for example, is used in the Funeral service, and not, as in the Holy Communion service, the 'Liturgy of the Word'.

The Gathering

[Sentences]
Introduction
[Prayer]
[Prayers of Penitence]
The Collect

Readings and Sermon

Prayers

Commendation and Farewell

The Committal

The Dismissal

(p. 258)

The Gathering

The sensitive gathering of the Funeral community is essential. Those who form the congregation at a Funeral service have at least one thing in common – their relationship with the deceased. They will not necessarily know all the other members of the congregation or be from the same local or family community. The minister conducting the service, and the building in which the Funeral is held, may or may not be familiar to the mourners. The service will be relatively short and the congregation will afterwards go their separate ways. In these circumstances, the various grieving needs of those attending the Funeral are best served by creating for that brief moment of time a (Christian) community which has assembled to say goodbye to someone who was important for them. That is the purpose of the Gathering.

The Funeral Service is an act of Christian worship. The mourners, or at least some of them, have gathered to express their faith as well as their feelings. In this respect, the Gathering attempts the creation of a Christian community focused on God in the presence of death. A life has ended that has been lived in the context of ultimate realities. In Christian eyes, there would be no purpose in the meeting were it not 'in the name of Jesus Christ, who died and was raised to the glory of God the Father'.

All the material in the Gathering section is there to enable these things to happen. The pastoral introduction explains the purpose of a Christian Funeral in helpfully straightforward language. The sentences, a well-established part of the Christian Funeral tradition, proclaim the note of spiritual solemnity as well as of Christian hope. Generations of people have risen to their feet with the Johannine words of Jesus ringing in their ears: 'I am the resurrection and the life, says the Lord . . .'.

> *The coffin may be received by the minister (see Note 7 on page 292). One or more sentences of Scripture may be used.*
>
> *(p. 259)*

Various suggestions relating to the reception of the coffin are listed in Note 7. Some of the suggestions are new; others honour or reform practices traditional to some within the Church. All suggestions, however, have the potential to meet pastoral needs as well as to give symbolic expression to aspects of Christian faith.

It is helpful to be reminded that 'The coffin may be received into the church at the beginning of the service, or earlier in the day, or on the day before the funeral'. So strong is the tradition of receiving the coffin at the beginning of the service, that bereaved families are frequently surprised to find that there are other possibilities. Many people have, for example, found real comfort in the knowledge that the deceased has 'come home' to rest in the church for the night before the funeral rather than remain in the undertaker's mortuary.

Note 7 makes various other imaginative suggestions:

- A candle may stand beside the coffin and may be carried in front of the coffin when it is brought into the church.

- The coffin may be sprinkled with water on entry. This may occur at the Commendation, or at the Committal.

- Family, friends or other members of the congregation may place a pall over the coffin in church. (A pall is a simple white cloth that signifies the baptismal status of the deceased.)

- Before or at the start of the service or after the opening prayer and hymn, and with the minister's agreement, suitable symbols of the life and faith of the departed person may be placed on or near the coffin.

- At the sprinkling, the placing of the pall or symbols, the words on pages 295–6 may be used.

The Supplementary Texts include some words for receiving the coffin, sprinkling the coffin with water, covering the coffin with a pall, and placing a Bible and a cross on the coffin. They helpfully communicate the meaning of the symbolic action. Such explanations might also be addressed with the family before the service and/or during the course of the sermon.

Introduction
When everyone has taken their place, there is a liturgical greeting (which does not require a spoken response) and then the minister

is given some words to welcome the congregation which reiterate briefly the purpose of the Funeral. (The minister may use other suitable words.) This is a new provision. Previous Anglican services have launched straight into prayers. The introduction is intended to help the congregation to be more at ease: it is personal, particular to the deceased person, and tells the mourners very briefly what is going to happen.

One or two prayers for the congregation may be said at this point, asking that God will comfort and encourage them in their time of grief. The first prayer is possibly the more appropriate one for a largely Christian congregation, the second for a more mixed gathering, possibly at a crematorium. These prayers address the grief, distress and shock of the mourners. The option to omit might perhaps be taken at Funerals where a practising Christian has died full of years, peacefully and 'in grace'.

> *A hymn may be sung.*
> *A brief tribute may be made.*

This reference to a 'tribute' is the first official liturgical mention of a practice that has been part of many Christian as well as secular Funerals for some time. The notes clarify the reference.

> Remembering and honouring the life of the person who has died, and the evidence of God's grace and work in them, should be done in the earlier part of the service, after the opening prayer, though if occasion demands it may be woven into the sermon or come immediately before the Commendation. It may be … spoken by a family member or friend … It is preferable not to interrupt the flow of the Reading(s) and Sermon with a tribute …
>
> *Note 4 (p. 291)*

The reference to a tribute, and its placing within the rite at this point, suggests that the acknowledgement of the deceased's earthly life and achievements might most appropriately come early in the service so that the biblical readings and sermon can move on to proclamation of the Christian hope.

Some ministers may prefer, however, perhaps especially at the Funeral of a practising Christian, to interweave the tribute with the sermon. The life of a Christian witnesses to their personal faith and trust in God, and so has the power to draw others to faith.

Whatever the positioning of the tribute, the encouragement to speak it aloud mercifully places our humanity in the context of God's providence and love. What is really important is our belief that the 'last word' on a person is always God's word.

Prayers of Penitence

At this point in the service, perhaps somewhat unexpectedly, there is the opportunity to include prayers of penitence. Penitence is a natural and necessary part of Christian worship, though it has not previously been our custom to include penitential prayers in the Funeral Service. As the Funeral Service focuses very much on human frailty, however, it is not unnatural for the situation to make us aware of our own shortcomings. The opportunity for penitence and reconciliation is therefore appropriate. Again, a Funeral always reminds us of our own mortality, and that raises questions for us as to our readiness to face God's final judgement.

It may seem that to position the act of penitence immediately after the tribute to the deceased is inappropriate. Note 4 allows for the tribute to be included within the sermon or placed immediately before the Commendation. Alternatively, the prayers of penitence may be included within the prayers of the people.

The Collect

The Collect is one of the essential texts. The set collect is a prayer, made in the presence of death, for a strengthening of the faith of the congregation that all who have died in the love of Christ will share in his resurrection.

The Resources section includes two alternative collects, both of which provide for the deceased to be mentioned by name. The first alternative simply adds the name of the deceased to the set collect. The second alternative collect prays for the benefits of Christ's saving passion and glorious resurrection for all, in company with the deceased person and all the faithful departed.

Readings and Sermon

The rubrics require that there be a psalm or hymn, a reading
from the New Testament and a sermon. The purpose of the
mandatory sermon is to proclaim the Gospel in the context of
the death of this particular person. There may be an additional
Scripture reading from the Old or New Testament. Psalm 23 is
printed in the main text. Some suggestions for Bible readings are
printed in full in the Resources section: a good number of
references, alternative bible readings and psalms are also given.

It is not unusual today for families to request that a secular
reading be used at a Funeral Service in addition to the biblical
readings. Christian opinion is divided as to the appropriateness
of setting biblical and secular readings alongside each other. If
the preference is to use only biblical readings at this point of the
service, suitable secular readings requested by the family could be
included earlier, at the time of the tribute.

Prayers

The rubric indicates that 'a minister' will lead the prayers of the
people. While this rubric helpfully encourages the active
participation of another person, lay or ordained, in the leading
of the service, it might seem to exclude an ordinary lay member
of the congregation from leading the prayers. In some
circumstances, however, the presiding minister might judge that a
lay church member, such as someone who had been visiting the
deceased regularly during their illness, might be the most
appropriate person to lead the prayers.

A suggested usual sequence of prayers is listed, allowing the
leader the freedom to construct a set of prayers appropriate for
the particular context.

- Thanksgiving for the life of the departed;

- Prayer for those who mourn;

- Prayers of penitence (if not already used);

- Prayer for readiness to live in the light of eternity.

The text of a short responsive form of intercessions is included. (The responses may be omitted).

The Lord's Prayer may be said at this point or immediately before the Dismissal.

Those whose custom it is to include prayer for the departed in the Funeral Service will find no prayers for the departed in the authorized Funeral material. The alternative prayers of entrusting and commending (Resources, p. 368) do contain five prayers for use 'at the time of death'. Those who see the Funeral as a recapitulation of the moment of death might consider these to be appropriate texts to use at this point.

Prayer for the departed remains a widely contentious issue in the life of the Church of England. The agreed *Common Worship* policy is that the authorized printed Funeral texts should only contain words and prayers that everyone should feel able to use. There is, however, freedom within the rubrics for ministers to choose and use the prayers they consider the most appropriate.

Commendation and Farewell

The Commendation is a prayer of entrusting the deceased person to God's merciful keeping. When the committal is to take place elsewhere, and in the presence of a smaller number of people, this prayer can also be seen as a focus for the end of a Funeral service in church.

There is one primary text for the Commendation. A good variety of alternative texts of entrusting and commending is given in the Resources section. This helpful selection includes appropriate forms for special circumstances. Commendations for the Funerals of infants and children are included within the Resources for the Funeral of a Child (pp. 312–13).

The Committal

The Committal immediately follows the Commendation except when it is to take place elsewhere. In these circumstances, the Commendation would be followed by the Dismissal.

The texts of the Committal are very similar to those in *The Alternative Service Book*. The two sets of verses from Psalm 103 are retained for use immediately before the Prayer of Committal. The second set has been slightly revised to be more inclusive ('we' instead of 'men') and it has one additional phrase that represents the full extent of the *Prayer Book* sentence.

Three forms of words are given for the Prayer of Committal. There is realism as to the widespread use of cremation. The first form is appropriate at the burial of a body, the thitd for committal in a crematorium. The second form provides for those occasions when ashes are buried in a churchyard or cemetery at some later date.

> We have entrusted our *brother/sister* N to God's mercy,
> and we now commit *his/her* body to the ground:
> earth to earth, ashes to ashes, dust to dust:
> in sure and certain hope of the resurrection to eternal life
> through our Lord Jesus Christ,
> who will transform our frail bodies
> that they may be conformed to his glorious body,
> who died, was buried, and rose again for us.
> To him be glory for ever.
>
> *(p. 269)*

In the form of words to be used at the crematorium before a later Burial of Ashes, we are encouraged to see the cremation as a preparation for burial.

> and now, in preparation for burial,
> we give *his/her* body to be cremated.
> We look for the fullness of the resurrection
> when Christ shall gather all his saints
> to reign with him in glory for ever.
>
> *(p. 269)*

The note relating to the Committal indicates that it should be used at the point at which it is needed. Interring the ashes as soon as possible after the cremation is commended, whether in churchyard, cemetery, vault, mausoleum or brick grave. Scattering or sprinkling ashes are nowhere authorized.

The Dismissal

One of the perceived weaknesses of *The Alternative Service Book* was the absence of a proper dismissal at the end of the Funeral Service. The *Common Worship* Funeral Service, however, sees the Dismissal as an integral and important part of the service. To that end, the choice of several well-known texts and prayers is given and the use of 'other suitable prayers' is allowed. It is suggested that, if it has not been used earlier, the Lord's Prayer might be said immediately after the Committal. A simple but powerful blessing text is given.

May God give *you*
his comfort and his peace,
his light and his joy,
in this world and the next;
and the blessing . . .

(p. 272)

The Funeral Service within a Celebration of Holy Communion

Structure

The Gathering
[Sentences]
[Introduction]
[Prayer]
Prayers of Penitence
The Collect

The Liturgy of the Word
Reading(s)
Gospel Reading
Sermon

Prayers

The Liturgy of the Sacrament
The Peace
Preparation of the Table
Taking of the Bread and Wine
The Eucharistic Prayer
The Lord's Prayer
Breaking of the Bread
Giving of Communion
Prayer after Communion

Commendation and Farewell

The Committal

The Dismissal

(p. 274)

It is appropriate, and indeed traditional, for the Funeral Service for regular communicants to be set in the context of a service of Holy Communion. Whether or not the context is also appropriate for all the deceased's family and friends has to be a matter for sensitive discussion between the deceased's minister and the next of kin. (Alternatively, the coffin may be brought into church earlier in the day or the night before, in time for a Holy Communion service to be celebrated before the Funeral Service. Those close to the deceased who are communicants often appreciate this provision.)

Common Worship gives a structure for a Funeral Service in the context of Holy Communion followed by the text of the service, excluding a few presidential texts (cross-reference for these is made to the main volume and President's edition of *Common Worship*). The texts of the service could be adapted for a service of Holy Communion to stand separately from the actual Funeral Service (for example, to be celebrated on the eve of the Funeral).

All the theological images in the texts resonate with the Easter hope of resurrection and new life. Most of the texts are familiar; others are new. Both the Gospel Acclamations and the introduction to the Peace use well-known Bible references, though none of these references actually echoes verses from the table of recommended Bible readings.

The Prayer at the Preparation of the Table encouragingly suggests the unity of the Church on earth with the Church in heaven.

> May all who are called to a place at your table
> follow in the way that leads to the unending feast of life.
>
> *(p. 283)*

There are three suggestions for a Proper Preface for the Eucharistic Prayer. The first is a repetition of a text from *The Alternative Service Book*; the second is a short new Easter preface, which points to Christ who is 'our hope of resurrection'; because of him 'The sting of death has been removed by the glorious promise of his risen life'. The third preface, again new, is a longer one with an optional congregational response, which would fit particularly well with Eucharistic Prayers A and E of *Common Worship*. The optional response, and the words preceding the Sanctus, enable the congregation, in the light of Christ's resurrection, to express its part in the worship of heaven, so joining their voices with the voice of their loved one who has died.

[With all your saints
we give you thanks and praise.]

The joy of resurrection fills the universe,
and so we join with angels and archangels,
with [*N and*] all your faithful people,
evermore praising you and *saying*:

(p. 284)

The new Prayer after Communion also expresses the theme of the
unity of life in Christ before and after death. It is a strong and
hopeful prayer that, while especially appropriate in the context of
a Funeral, could also be used as a post communion prayer on
other occasions.

Gracious God,
we thank you that in your great love
you have fed us with the spiritual food and drink
    of the body and blood of your Son Jesus Christ
and have given us a foretaste of your heavenly banquet:
grant that this sacrament may be to us
a comfort in affliction
and a pledge of our inheritance
in that kingdom where there is no death,
neither sorrow nor crying,
but fullness of joy with all your saints;

(p. 286)

Notes

The notes to the services follow after the primary texts, as do the
notes in all the *Common Worship* services. Placed at the end of
the service text, rather than at the beginning, as was the case in
The Alternative Service Book, they do not distract the
worshippers. The notes are for the minister, and helpfully amplify
the options with regard to the Sentences, Psalms and Readings,
Hymns, the Tribute, the Sermon, the Creed, the Receiving of the
Coffin, the Committal and The Funeral Service within a
Celebration of Holy Communion.

Supplementary Texts

Sentences

Sentences, short verses from Scripture, have traditionally been used to begin Anglican services, to introduce the offertory at Holy Communion, and to be said or sung during processions. The *Common Worship* provision for prayers and services around the time of death has been imaginative in developing other ways of encouraging this way of praying in our worship.

There is a veritable feast of additional sentences at the beginning of the Supplementary Texts for Funerals. What is their purpose? Traditionally, for Funerals, the sentences have effectively covered the processions in and out of church, chapel and crematorium. The words 'I am the resurrection and the life, says the Lord' are a clear 'stand up now' signal to Anglican congregations. People know that these words mark the beginning of the Funeral Service. No other sentence has that power.

The Book of Common Prayer provided just three sentences at the beginning of the Burial Order; *The Alternative Service Book* expanded the provision to eight; the main *Common Worship* Funeral Service has reduced this to seven, but has added twenty-one in this additional selection.

In the Pastoral Services surrounding death, *Common Worship* suggests various other ways in which scriptural sentences can be used. The Preparation section for 'Ministry at the Time of Death', for example, lists a good number of spiritually helpful short texts to be repeated gently with the dying person. The 'Prayer when Someone has Just Died' uses a couple of biblical sentences as a gentle assurance of consolation. These could be said slowly, dropping gently into the silence around the dead person. The Word of God section 'At Home after the Funeral' is effectively a choice from several 'long' biblical sentences. Another set of sentences is suggested for the Funeral of a Child. Each set of sentences is slightly different – the sentences being selected according to the spiritual and pastoral needs of the situation.

These are all ways of using Scripture 'out of context', and some might question the validity of this. It is true, however, that as spiritual human beings we 'latch on' to certain words of Scripture because, in all sorts of contexts, they are powerful for us. What we are being given here are more 'words of power' with which to feel ourselves in touch with God, and more circumstances in which they can be used helpfully.

From the selection given in this resource, and at other points in the Funeral Services, we are free to use those sentences we feel most appropriate for a given situation, and with which we ourselves feel most at ease.

Some Texts which may be used by the Minister

The texts given are for: Receiving the coffin; Sprinkling the coffin with water; Covering the coffin with a pall; Placing a Bible on the coffin; Placing a cross on the coffin. (See also Notes 4 and 7.)

• Receiving the coffin

> We receive the body of our *brother/sister N*
> with confidence in God, the giver of life,
> who raised the Lord Jesus from the dead.
>
> *(p. 295)*

The words to accompany the receiving of the coffin are particularly useful for saying at the church gate or entrance, before the procession into the church building. They give dignity to that often awkward little moment when the minister feels the need to ask the undertaker, 'Are you ready?'

• Sprinkling the coffin with water

The suggested action of sprinkling the coffin with water relates to the baptismal status of the deceased, and is only appropriate for those who have been baptized.

Two texts are given. The first, being shorter, and therefore more easily memorized, might well be used when the coffin is received at the church door. The second, longer text, with its reference to burial, might be more appropriate for use at a service of interment. It can be said before the Committal.

There is no need to restrict this symbolic action of sprinkling water to those churches that possess a sprinkler or aspergilium.[1] A small part of a tree branch is a very effective alternative; a green-leafed twig has an appropriate 'new life' or 'everlasting life' symbolism about it.

> With this water we call to mind *N*'s baptism.
> As Christ went through the deep waters of death for us,
> so may he bring us to the fullness of resurrection life
> with *N* and all the redeemed.
>
> *(or)*
>
> Grant, Lord,
> that we who are baptized into the death
>   of your Son our Saviour Jesus Christ
> may continually put to death our evil desires
>   and be buried with him;
> and that through the grave and gate of death
> we may pass to our joyful resurrection;
> through his merits,
> who died and was buried and rose again for us,
> your Son Jesus Christ our Lord.
>
> *(p. 295)*

● Covering the coffin with a pall

In the Church of England, we are perhaps unused to using a
Funeral pall, and may be somewhat apprehensive of unfamiliar
imagery. But the Funeral pall symbolizes the Christian's white
baptismal garment, and so is another proclamation of the
baptismal status of the deceased. (Like the sprinkling with water,
therefore, this symbolic action is also appropriate only for those
who have been baptized.)

> We are already God's children,
> but what we shall be has not yet been revealed.
> Yet we know that when Christ appears we shall be like him,
> for we shall see him as he is.
>
> *(or)*
>
> On Mount Zion the Lord will remove the pall of sorrow
> hanging over all nations.
> He will destroy death for ever.
> He will wipe away the tears from every face.
>
> *(p. 295)*

- Placing a Bible on the coffin

- Placing a cross on the coffin

These two symbolic actions and the words that accompany them speak of the love of God for his children in giving them his word, and in dying for them on the cross.

> Lord Jesus Christ,
> your living and imperishable word brings us to new birth.
> Your eternal promises to us and to N are proclaimed in the
>   Bible.
>
> Lord Jesus Christ,
> for love of N and each one of us
> you bore our sins on the cross.
>
> *(p. 296)*

The Blessing of a Grave

We are given a very useful text for the blessing of a grave. Even in situations where the ground is already consecrated, there can be something pastorally very helpful about being able to say a prayer such as this with members of the deceased's family on the day of or in the hours before the Funeral.

The Burial of Ashes

In *The Alternative Service Book*, the form of words for use at 'the interment of the Ashes' was rather brief. While it is true that the Funeral Service has already taken place, the Burial of Ashes is, for the mourners, an emotionally necessary ritual that completes the Funeral Service. After a cremation, the Burial of Ashes is the Committal; and it necessarily takes place on a separate occasion.

In theory, few words are necessary. The pastoral need, however, is for something a little more substantial, particularly if the ceremony has had to be delayed for some reason. *Common Worship* responds well to these pastoral needs. While the service is not a long one, it is a service. Provision is made for the ceremony to begin in a church or chapel and to proceed to the place of burial at the end of the Scripture readings.

The service has a distinct beginning, middle and end. The suggested words after the greeting encapsulate the spiritual context and purpose neatly:

> Though we are dust and ashes
> God has prepared for those who love him
>   a heavenly dwelling place.
> At *his/her* funeral we commended N into the hands
>   of almighty God.
> As we prepare to commit the remains of N to the earth
> we entrust ourselves and all who love God
>   to his loving care.
>
> *(p. 323)*

Sentences may follow the introduction and there should be one or more Scripture readings (the full text of six readings is printed) before the Committal. After the Committal, the Lord's Prayer and other prayers are said. Two such prayers are given; other prayers may be inserted between them. The service ends with a prayer of dismissal.

The minister may instinctively opt to use the first of the two Committal prayers as it is the more familiar prayer, with its powerful use of traditional 'earth to earth, ashes to ashes, dust to dust' imagery and language. The alternative prayer, however, is well worth considering. It is a new prayer, which imaginatively mixes together various biblical images relating to creation and love.

> God our Father,
> in loving care your hand has created us,
> and as the potter fashions the clay
> you have formed us in your image.
> Through the Holy Spirit
> you have breathed into us the gift of life.
> In the sharing of love you have enriched our knowledge
>   of you and of one another.
> We claim your love today,
> as we return these ashes to the ground
> in sure and certain hope of the resurrection to eternal life.
>
> *(p. 328)*

This might be a particularly suitable prayer for one member of a married couple; it might also be a prayer that someone would choose to plan into their own Funeral. I suspect that a minister who does choose to use this prayer might well be tempted to insert the 'dust to dust' phrase in between the last two lines.

Of the two prayers that immediately follow the Committal, the first might usefully be printed on a card and given to mourners for their use on subsequent visits to the grave.

> Heavenly Father,
> we thank you for all those whom we love but see no longer.
> As we remember N in this place,
> hold before us our beginning and our ending,
> the dust from which we come
> and the death to which we move,
> with a firm hope in your eternal love and purposes for us,
> in Jesus Christ our Lord.
>
> *(p. 330)*

Authorized alternative prayers

The following authorized alternative texts are printed in the Resources section.

The symbolism is also very personal in that normally the deceased person's own Bible and cross will be used. It can be a simple yet very moving way of involving members of the deceased's family or friends in the ceremony, and may well be particularly helpful in enabling younger family members to contribute.

At most Funerals flowers cover the coffin. For a Christian, the two symbols of Bible and cross speak powerfully of the eternal and imperishable love of God, and so complement the perishable floral symbols of human affection.

A practical question does arise: what shall we do with the Bible and cross after the Funeral? At some Funerals it will be appropriate that the Bible and cross be buried or cremated with the coffin. At other services, that may not feel right; indeed sometimes the deceased person's Bible and cross will have been gifted to relatives or friends.

Collects

The main collect prays for blessings on the congregation. Two alternative collects are given in the Resources section. The first alternative collect is effectively the same as the primary collect, but it does allow for the deceased to be mentioned by name. The second prayer is a slightly revised version of the more solemn *Alternative Service Book* collect. It too refers to the deceased by name, and can be used to bear the spiritual intentions of those who wish to pray for the deceased at their Funeral.

The Authorized Prayers of Entrusting and Commending

There is quite a wide selection of Prayers of Entrusting and Commending which can be found in the Resources section. The last four of these prayers may well provide helpful alternatives for those who feel strongly about the importance of prayers for the departed. Prayers of commendation particularly appropriate for the death of an infant, a stillbirth or miscarriage are included in the Resources for the Funeral of a Child.

Posture

The authorized texts, with the Notes and Supplementary Texts, together with the other commended Resources, are extremely comprehensive. We have been given very adequate provision for most circumstances. The many options and additional resources allow for different shades of theological understanding as well as for various pastoral situations. In addition, all the possibilities for personalizing the service are extremely welcome.

The only omission (and, to be fair, it has always been an omission) relates to questions of posture. Instructions about whether to sit, kneel or stand are left entirely to the discretion of the minister. But posture is very important, not just theologically but also for reasons of comfort. All ministers will have worked out their own local tried and tested patterns of posture with the Funeral Services hitherto used. There are, however, differences between *The Alternative Service Book* and *Common Worship* services, that necessitate a reassessment of practice. Other factors govern the posture of the congregation. They include the building itself, the style of seating, which way the seats face, and whether it is possible to kneel. In addition the age of the congregation may need to be taken into consideration. For all these reasons, posture instructions need to be thought out as carefully as the selection of the texts. It is also helpful, especially in the case of a Funeral service in the crematorium, if the Funeral director is aware of the normal practice of the minister.

Funerals normally take place either in a crematorium or in a church. The former is the more difficult to stage effectively. At the beginning of the service, a significant number of people will follow the coffin into the building. Those already inside the building will stand; but often those who follow the coffin in may kneel or sit when they come into their places. The minister, who may well have been saying the sentences, may therefore need to ask everyone to stand for the Greeting and the first part of the service. (Though if the chief mourners are old and very distressed, it may be kinder to get everyone to sit for most of the service.)

Depending on the style and orientation of seats and pews, a short crematorium service might normally be choreographed in this way:

Stand

    Entry

    Greeting and Introduction

    (Hymn)

    Collect

Sit

    Bible Reading

    Sermon

Sit/Kneel

    Prayers

Stand

    (Hymn)

    Commendation

    Committal

    Dismissal

A church Funeral gives more scope for movement and posture as well as more time. A full Funeral service which included all the options suggested in *Common Worship* might be ordered thus:

Stand

    Entry

    Greeting and Introduction

    Prayer

    (First Hymn)

Sit

    Tribute

Kneel/sit

> Prayers of Penitence
>
> Collect

Sit

> Bible Readings
>
> Sermon

Kneel/sit

> Prayers

Stand

> (Hymn)
>
> Commendation
>
> Committal
>
> Dismissal

Posture is not the only consideration when it comes to thinking about how best to use the building. In Chapter 5, 'The Funeral Service', we address other issues relating to the Funeral environment.

Theological proclamation and pastoral care

The words offered to the Church by the authorized *Common Worship* Funeral Services, together with the optional supplementary texts, balance a strong theological proclamation in the face of death with sensitive spiritual and pastoral care for those who mourn. Great care has been taken to honour the breadth of theological understanding that is held within the Church of England. As well as the basic text for the Funeral Service, we have the additional helpful resource of an almost complete text for a Funeral Service in the context of Holy Communion. Many will appreciate this provision.

The next chapter explores the wide variety of further commended material in *Common Worship*: Ministry at the Time of Death; Before the Funeral; The Order for a Funeral of a Child; After the Funeral; Prayers, Bible Readings and Canticles for use at Funeral and Memorial Services.

Note

1. The technical term 'aspergilium' derives from the verb used in the Latin (Vulgate) translation of Psalm 51.7, 'Thou shalt sprinkle me with hyssop and I shall be clean: and I shall be made whiter than snow'. In the Roman rite these words may still be recited when holy water is sprinkled over the people, in a symbolic action with its probable origin in the early rites of exorcism. In the Easter Vigil Service, however, there is a reference to the sprinkling of the people with water in the ancient prayer of blessing the baptismal water. Over the centuries, this action has become a reminder not so much of forgiveness but of baptism, and is seen as a means of renewing baptismal grace. This is why in many churches today, on Easter Eve, after the people have renewed their baptismal vows, they are sprinkled with water to symbolize their baptismal renewal. When, therefore, the *Common Worship* Funeral Service suggests that the coffin of a baptized Christian might be sprinkled with water, it is drawing from this latter tradition. There is no intention at all that this action should be seen purely as a symbol of absolution.

3 The commended Funeral material: Services Before and After the Funeral, Prayers and other resources

A wide breadth of liturgical provision

In addition to the main Funeral services, *Common Worship* includes further supportive material for the Church's pastoral care of the dying and the bereaved, thus offering a breadth of liturgical provision and care. Even a quick look at the various title-page summaries gives some helpful prompts for those who try to bring spiritual comfort and support to people who are having to cope with death, either their own impending death or someone else's.

A Summary of the Provisions

Ministry at the Time of Death

   Preparation

   Reconciliation

   Opening Prayer

   The Word of God

   Prayers

   Laying on of Hands and Anointing

Memorial Service: a Sample Service

The Gathering

Readings and Sermon

Prayers

The Commendation

The Dismissal

Conclusion

Prayers for Use with the Dying and at Funeral and Memorial Services

Prayers with Dying People

Gathering Prayers

Prayers of Penitence (Kyries and Absolutions)

Collects

Thanksgiving for the Life of the Departed

Prayers for Those who Mourn

Prayers for Readiness to live in the Light of Eternity

Litanies and Responsive Prayers

Prayers of Entrusting and Commending

Blessings and other Endings

Prayers for use after Psalms.

There are also Bible Readings, Psalms and Canticles for use at Funeral and Memorial Services.

The commended texts

Ministry at the Time of Death

'Ministry at the Time of Death' is a relatively new title for Church of England services. (It was first used in 1991.) In 1983, a supplement to *The Alternative Service Book* was published. Entitled 'Ministry to the Sick', it provided services and prayers commended for use with sick and dying people. It included Communion with the Sick; The Laying on of Hands with Prayer and Anointing; A Commendation at the Time of Death; and Prayers for use with the Sick. An Appendix offered Psalms and Readings.

Common Worship provision has separated 'Ministry to the Sick' from 'Ministry at the Time of Death', rightly recognizing these as two distinctive ministries. 'Ministry at the Time of Death' complements the Funeral rites and gives us worship and prayers for use with those who are dying and with the bereaved. Services and prayers for the Church's ministry to the sick are now included in the provision for *Wholeness and Healing*.

Most people hope to die peacefully at home, and perhaps the most natural flow of the services and prayers at the time of death in *Common Worship* relates to this situation.

Bernard, as a Christian doctor, was familiar with most aspects of the Church's ministry at the time of death. When he was diagnosed as having a terminal illness, he expected his parish priest to help him prepare for death and to use the appropriate services and prayers. The first time of worship he and his priest had together was a service of Holy Communion at his hospital bedside after his diagnosis and initial operation. They acknowledged aloud in the prayers together the terminal nature of his illness. The priest laid hands on him. For three or four months, he recovered enough strength to live normally at home and to come to church on Sundays. He was determined to live his life as fully as possible, and was not prepared to die until he had to! He talked a lot to his children at that time, which meant a lot to them. Towards the end, he discussed his Funeral with them, and the disposal of his ashes. Bernard was not accustomed to private confession, but during that time, conversations with his priest led to extemporary prayers which covered many aspects of his life, including the acknowledgement of things he was sorry for. The laying on of hands was regularly given. When the time of death drew near, Bernard waited until very near the end before he asked his family to ring for the priest. That night, his family gathered round his bed. The priest used the prayers for Ministry at the Time of Death from the Opening Prayer through to the Commendation and Blessing. The family was with him as well as the priest. Bernard had not said anything for some time, but when the priest anointed him, he did raise his hand to his brow and said 'Amen'. The priest and family shared Holy Communion together, then the priest said a prayer of commendation and blessing, and left the family to keep watch. (They had copies of the *Common Worship* prayers and used them quietly as they watched with Bernard.) Bernard died in the early hours of the morning. The priest rejoined the family after breakfast. The prayers for 'when someone has just died' were said around Bernard's bed. The family then sent for the undertaker. All felt they had done 'what Dad would have wanted', and this gave them a sense of peace within their grief.

The texts provided for Ministry at the Time of Death enable the parish minister to lead people gently and gracefully forward in the spiritual journey towards death. We begin with the acknowledgement of our own sinfulness and the assurance of God's forgiveness. We are taken, by way of hearing God's word in Scripture and our own response in faith and prayer, to God's gifts in the laying on of hands and anointing. The final stage of the journey is our communion with the risen Lord.

Not all deaths, however, are gentle or in bed. But to say a prayer with someone who is dying, in whatever circumstances, is to bring the love and grace of God to a distressing and shocking situation. In the case of an accident or sudden death, a priest or minister may wish to say one or two short prayers, such as the

Kyries, the Lord's Prayer and a prayer of committal. Even after someone has actually died, it is quite appropriate to say the Lord's Prayer and a prayer of committal. Although ministers can, and sometimes have to extemporize, there are commendation prayers in *Common Worship* that can be learnt off by heart. The Nunc Dimittis can also be used as a prayer of committal.

> When Philip died suddenly, his minister was one of those who found him. While the family was telephoning the ambulance, the minister was able quietly to kneel by Philip's body and say the Kyries, the Lord's Prayer and as much as she could remember of the prayer 'Go forth, O Christian soul'.

When someone has died suddenly, some of the prayers in 'Ministry at the Time of Death' can also be used with the family at an appropriate moment after the death. (Shock at sudden death, however, may mean that formal prayer is inappropriate until, say, the conclusion of the minister's first visit.) For some Christian families, it may be helpful to share the service of Holy Communion with them, but not until after the first shock has begun to recede.

Note

There is a positive encouragement to the minister to be open about the imminence of death. There is an important place for 'private' preparation.

> The person should be helped to be aware that the time of death is approaching.
>
> *(p. 217)*

For the Christian, penitence and reconciliation are a very important part of such preparation. While the ministry of reconciliation is preferably exercised in private, the note encourages the presence of close friends and family for the following prayers, and especially at the time of Holy Communion.

The point is made that ministry at the time of death does not necessarily happen all at once, but may be spread out over some days or weeks. The last Holy Communion, for example, may be received on another occasion 'and more than once, as pastoral necessity dictates.'

Preparation

A number of short texts, one or more of which may be repeated softly with someone who is dying, are printed in full. The Lord's Prayer follows. The intention is to prepare the person who is dying for the ministry of reconciliation.

The texts are all biblical, from both Old and New Testaments. They are all affirmative of Christian faith. The wide provision allows the minister to choose those words that seem to be particularly appropriate to the spiritual need of the dying person. When, for example, death is seen to be near, the repetition of a text such as 'Lord Jesus, receive my spirit' can be offered for the dying person to make their own, and indeed for them to accept that they have 'permission' to let go of life.

Reconciliation

This section of the prayers before death provides for 'some expression of penitence' and for the assurance of God's forgiveness. A couple of penitential prayers are given and the threefold Kyries. The shorter prayers are particularly helpful in that they could be repeated two or three times, thus giving the person who is dying the opportunity to join in. Two forms of absolution are given: one for use by a priest, possibly with the laying on of hands; the other for use by a deacon or lay person.

Opening Prayer

While the ministry of preparation and reconciliation is intimate and private, it is good to be encouraged to gather those close to the dying person around the bedside at this point, so that they can support him or her with their prayers. There are many touches in the rubrics and prayers that follow which affirm this important ministry from family and close friends.

Wherever someone is dying becomes a 'holy space', whether it be at home, in hospital or in a hospice. The prayers and symbolic actions that are suggested serve to reinforce that sense of holiness. For some, the initial reaction to praying aloud with a dying person may be that it would be more 'comfortable' at home. It is perfectly possible, however, to create an intimate and holy space around a hospital or hospice bed, and what is offered in these texts helps people do just that.

People often need positive encouragement to watch with their dying friend or relative. The opening prayers are gentle in their ministry not only to the person who is dying but also to those who watch with them. The prayers enable feelings of diffidence and fear in the presence of imminent death to be faced. They help people perceive death in the context of the promise of eternal life. The suggested opening prayer is a very strengthening one.

Eternal God,
grant to your servant
(and to us who surround *him/her* with our prayers)
your peace beyond our understanding.
Give us faith, the comfort of your presence,
and the words to say to one another and to you,
as we gather in the name of Jesus Christ our Lord.

(p. 222)

The Word of God

Three appropriate Scripture readings are suggested, and it would be helpful to have the complete texts to hand. This is a good opportunity to involve a family member or a friend. Other Bible passages may be used. Those who watch, or the person who is dying, may well want to read or hear a favourite Scripture passage which feels appropriate in the particular circumstances.

After the reading, the minister may encourage an act of faith or commitment. Four short single sentence affirmations are given, all in the first person singular. These sentences could be repeated several times, giving the dying person the opportunity to make the affirmation their own.

The use of the first person singular in the words of affirmation could feel strange to those who are gathered around the dying person. The minister might perhaps explain that a part of their prayerful support is vicarious. They are affirming Christian faith and praying on behalf of the dying person, who can no longer say things aloud him- or herself. This is also an opportunity for everyone present to say 'I believe' together. The little group gathered around the bed is a 'faith support group' both for the dying person and also for each other. In these very intimate and personal circumstances, there is a constant mixture of individual and corporate worship and spiritual need that has to be held together by the minister.

Prayers

This is also a time to pray for the person who is dying. The minister may either use the short litany given in the text, other prayers from the prayer resource pages, or pray in their own words. Both the litany and the short prayer given encourage all to join in the prayers.

The suggestion that everyone around the bed might join in the prayers, however, points up the need for the minister to have several copies of a prayer or worship leaflet to hand, containing a key selection of texts for ministry at the time of death. Such a leaflet would bring two benefits. Not only can family and friends join in with the prayers or play a part in the reading of Scripture, they can also use the leaflet in their own private prayers, as well as in their prayer vigil with their loved one who is dying. Suggestions for such a worship leaflet are given in Chapter 7.

The printed litany in the prayers will encourage and support those who find comfort and strength in solemn, traditional words that address the nearness of death and its spiritual challenge. It is important that we put the needs of the dying person first, and pray in such a way that they, if still in a state when words can be heard, feel included. The responses in this litany are familiar ones, and those used to praying in this way will know them off by heart. And the formality helps too by its very objectivity; emotions are focused.

The alternative that is suggested to the solemn litany is that the minister should pray aloud using his or her own words. The minister will probably base the choice of prayer style on what they perceive to be the feelings and spiritual needs of the person who is dying. What prayers will help that particular person most at the moment of their death? Formal words and known prayers, or informal extemporary prayer? People's spiritual needs and preferences do vary and ministers will want to honour them.

Common Worship provides a choice of styles and so encourages ministers to think more creatively about their ministry at the time of death. It might well be, for example, that someone to whom the ministry of music had been very important in life would be greatly helped by some music being played to them during their last hours. On the other hand, someone who enjoyed a more traditional Anglican liturgy in life would be more responsive to traditional Anglican prayers and responses in their movement towards death.

One of the more 'catholic' members of the Liturgical Commission, for example, described to a public audience his nightmare fears that the minister easing him through his last moments might only be able to come up with the words of 'Shine, Jesus, shine'. It was, of course, meant as a joke, but the provision made in these rites should go some way towards easing such anxieties.

Laying on of Hands and Anointing
The symbolic actions of the laying on of hands and the anointing with oil are practical expressions of our prayers for our dying brother or sister. For many people, touch can be an important means of allaying fear and feeling comforted. The words of the prayer make it clear that the priest or minister may administer the laying on of hands with prayer either on their own or with others.

In the name of our Lord Jesus Christ
I/we lay *my/our* hands on you, N.
May the Lord in his mercy and love uphold you
by the grace and power of the Holy Spirit.
May he deliver you from all evil,
give you light and peace,
and bring you to everlasting life.

(p. 226)

A priest should anoint, using oil that has been consecrated for the purpose (cf. Note 2 to the services, p. 232). Clear instructions are given in the text of the service as to how and where to anoint: 'making the sign of the cross in oil on his or her forehead and hands'.

> N, I anoint you with oil in the name of our Lord Jesus Christ.
> May the Lord in his love and mercy uphold you
> by the grace and power of the Holy Spirit.
>
> *(p. 226)*

The continuing words of the prayer of anointing given are strong ones and affirm the mercy of God. If there has been no previous opportunity for the dying person to make an act of penitence and to receive absolution, this prayer could be particularly appropriate.

> As you are outwardly anointed with this holy oil,
> so may our heavenly Father grant you the inward anointing
>   of the Holy Spirit.
> Of his great mercy
> may he forgive you your sins
> and release you from suffering.
> May he deliver you from all evil,
> preserve you in all goodness,
> and bring you to everlasting life;
> through Jesus Christ our Lord.
>
> *(p. 226)*

Holy Communion

> *If it is possible, the dying person may receive communion. Unless the bread and wine have already been consecrated, an authorized Eucharistic Prayer is used.*
>
> *(p. 227)*

It is recommended that those family and friends who are praying with the dying person should receive Holy Communion with them (see the Note on p. 217). Nothing is said in the notes to the service as to what might be done if the dying person is not physically able to receive the sacrament. But when those who are surrounding the dying person with their presence and prayers are themselves communicants, it can be particularly meaningful for them to share together in Holy Communion with the minister at this time, even if the dying person is not able to receive the bread and wine themselves. Again, many will also see such an act of Holy Communion as a vicarious one.

In the absence of a priest, an episcopally authorized lay minister may give communion from bread and wine which have been consecrated at a previous service of Holy Communion.

Commendation

The Lord's Prayer is said first, and then three sets of texts of commendation are given.

> *The minister speaks first to the dying person, using these or other suitable words*
>
> *(p. 229)*

The first commendation is addressed directly to the dying person. There is a choice of three texts, all of which will resonate as versions of prayers that have been traditionally used in the Church's ministry with the dying. They may be used at any time while someone is dying, and would be particularly powerful while the dying person is still aware of what is being said to him or her. (Other suitable words may be found in the authorized prayers of entrusting and commending.)

> *N*, go forth upon your journey from this world,
> in the name of God the Father almighty who created you;
> in the name of Jesus Christ who suffered death for you;
> in the name of the Holy Spirit who strengthens you;
> in communion with the blessed saints,
> and aided by angels and archangels,
> and all the armies of the heavenly host.
> May your portion be this day in peace,
> and your dwelling the heavenly Jerusalem.
>
> *(Second text, p. 229)*

The minister says the prayer of commendation

(p. 230)

The second set of commendation prayers offers two texts. The second prayer appears as an alternative commendation prayer in the Prayers of Entrusting and Commending (Resources and Prayers section). In the context of prayer with the dying, both these prayers have a slightly different thrust from those addressed to the dying person. They address God, and, while commending the dying person to God, they also address the needs of those who watch with the dying person. These are prayers said by others for the dying person, rather than a direct encouragement to the dying person to 'go forth' with God.

Gracious God,
nothing in death or life,
nothing in the world as it is,
nothing in the world as it shall be,
nothing in all creation
can separate us from your love.
Jesus commended his spirit into your hands at his last hour.
Into those same hands we now commend your servant N,
that dying to the world, and cleansed from sin,
death may be for *him/her* the gate to life
and to eternal fellowship with you . . .

(First text, p. 230)

One or more of the following may also be used

(p. 231)

The third set of commendations is more general. They include the Nunc Dimittis, the Russian Kontakion and St Anselm's 'Song of Christ's Goodness'. Even if it is felt that no more words need be said after the initial Commendation, these texts are helpful prayer resources for those who continue to watch with a dying person after the minister has left.

Anselm's 'Song of Christ's Goodness' is suggested for use at or just after death.

> Jesus, like a mother you gather your people to you;
> you are gentle with us as a mother with her children . . .
>
> You comfort us in sorrow and bind up our wounds . . .
>
> Lord Jesus, in your mercy heal us;
> in your love and tenderness remake us.
>
> In your compassion bring grace and forgiveness,
> for the beauty of heaven may your love prepare us.
>
> *(p. 232)*

Blessing

There should be a blessing; two forms are given. Both are words of blessing for everyone present. The first is a lovely prayer that a lay person could use; the second, a blessing taken from the eucharistic provision in *The Alternative Service Book*.

> May the eternal God
> bless and keep us,
>   guard our bodies,
> save our souls
>   and bring us safe
> to the heavenly country,
>   our eternal home,
> where Father, Son and Holy Spirit reign,
> one God for ever and ever.
>
> *(First blessing, p. 233)*

Prayer when someone has just died

> *The minister, a family member or friend, may use some or all of these words*
>
> *(p. 234)*

These prayers helpfully conclude the ministry at the time of death. They can be incorporated in a parish leaflet for this ministry, and so given to those who will watch with the dying person through to their death (see Chapter 7).

Notes

The four notes are of particular practical value to the clergy.

1. The first note gives advice with respect to the laying on of hands and to the giving of the Holy Communion when the minister is neither a bishop nor a priest. An alternative form of words for prayer with the laying on of hands is given, and the instruction: 'The Holy Communion may be given but not celebrated'.

2. The laying on of hands may be done by more than one person.

3. The practical advice given with respect to the oil used for anointing includes a prayer to be said by the priest over unconsecrated oil.

4. The fourth note reminds the minister to use 'versions of texts familiar to the dying person'.

The notes go some way towards giving practical support for the minister who, in these circumstances, always has to think on his or her feet – an essential element of this kind of ministry when every situation is different. The texts have the potential of flexible use but familiarity with the material provided will be essential for using it creatively as well as sensitively.

At Home before the Funeral

Note

The note indicates that the short service at home before the Funeral is flexible enough to be used either on hearing the news of a death, or as part of the minister's visit to the family before the Funeral. Either way the service could be led by a lay person: a family member, a friend, or a representative from the church. It is suggested that hymns might be sung at appropriate points.

Preparation

The words of preparation affirm the faith of those present that 'the Lord is in our midst' and that he comforts us. A short responsory is given. (Again, a simple service sheet would be helpful if the responsory prayers are to be used and if it is desired to give some more formal structure to the occasion. If what is preferred is something more relaxed and informal, the responsory could be omitted or used as a reading.)

Readings

The texts of three short Bible readings are given in full, but other appropriate readings may be used.

Prayers

Opportunity is given to share memories of the departed. Four prayers are given; they can either follow such a sharing of memories or stand on their own. It is quite likely, for example, that memories will have been shared informally before the time of prayer. If the minister was part of such a sharing, he or she might like to make reference to this before saying the prayers.

The fourth prayer should help the mourners move on to the next stage of the day.

> Lord, be with us as we open the door.
> Come in with us, go out with us.
> Do not sleep when we sleep,
> but watch over us, protect us and keep us safe,
> our only helper and maker.
>
> *(p. 239)*

This would also be an appropriate prayer to give to or to use with those who will return to an 'empty' home. It might even be printed out as a prayer card and given to someone to use as they adjust to life without the presence of the departed.

Conclusion

The Conclusion combines old and new phrases to create a prayer for light to break through the darkness of grief.

> And now to him who is able to keep us from falling,
> and lift us from the dark valley of despair
> to the bright mountain of hope,
> from the midnight of desperation
> to the daybreak of joy;
> to him be power and authority, for ever and ever.
>
> *(p. 239)*

For those Unable to be Present at the Funeral

The short service, which is deliberately based on the Funeral
Service, addresses the pastoral needs of mourners who for
whatever reason are not able to attend the Funeral. It could be
used on the same day as the Funeral, and possibly at about the
same time. There may be relatives who are prevented by distance
from attending the Funeral, or who are infirm or ill. A hospital
chaplain might use the prayers with a bereaved person who is in
hospital. Those who have stayed behind preparing food for the
people who are attending the Funeral might say the prayers
together.

A full text for this service is not given, except for the Gathering
and Prayers. The service leader is directed to the Funeral Service
for the Reading, Prayers, Commendation and Farewell.

Note
The note specifically encourages leadership by a friend or family
member. Parishes might usefully create their own leaflet version
of the service to assist a lay leader (see Chapter 7).

The Gathering
Full texts for the Gathering and opening prayers are given. The
Funeral bidding is adapted:

> We join with those in (*place*)
> in remembering before God our *brother/sister N* . . .
>
> (*p. 240*)

There is an opportunity for people to share memories of the
deceased, and a suggestion that the Penitential Prayers and
Collect from the Funeral Service might be used.

Reading
The leader chooses an appropriate reading from those suggested
for the Funeral Service.

Prayers

Depending upon the circumstances, the prayers used may either be those from the Funeral Service, or less formal material.

Commendation and Farewell

The words of the Commendation in the Funeral service may be adapted with the addition of a phrase such as 'With those in *(place)*' before the words, 'We entrust . . .' or 'We commend . . .'.

The service ends with a time of silence, the Lord's Prayer and a dismissal.

Receiving the Coffin at Church before the Funeral

There are circumstances when it feels right and proper for the deceased to rest in church through the night before the Funeral, or to be brought to church early on the day of the Funeral.

This service therefore helpfully provides for the reception of the coffin at church. It may be attended by a small number of those closest to the deceased; it may be a simple reception by the minister, possibly supported by one or two church members.

Receiving the coffin at the church door

The moment of arriving at church is a significant one, and it is good to be given simple but appropriate words to say.

> We receive the body of our *brother/sister N*
> with confidence in God, the giver of life,
> who raised the Lord Jesus from the dead.
>
> *(p. 242)*

Provision is then made for sprinkling the coffin with water, in remembrance of the deceased's baptism; suitable words are suggested. This could be done either at the church gate or at the entry into the church building. A selection of sentences is given, which could be used at any point as the coffin is being carried into the church, and there is a prayer to be said as the coffin is set down. At this point, there is an opportunity to place symbolic religious symbols on the coffin, such as a pall, a Bible or a cross, or, with the minister's permission, other suitable symbols of the life and faith of the deceased person (cf. the section on 'Symbols' in Chapter 5). If it feels appropriate for those present to 'share briefly their memories of the one who has died', this would be an appropriate moment to do so, possibly followed by a time of silence.

Readings and Prayers

If the ceremony of reception is to be kept relatively short, it might simply conclude with a prayer for the mourners, a Scripture reading, another prayer and an ending prayer. It may be, however, that a longer watch with the deceased is appropriate – for example, an overnight vigil. A good choice of prayers and readings is given in the order for a vigil.

Ending

The prayers that conclude the reception of the coffin encourage the mourners to leave the deceased in church and to move on, taking comfort from the love of God and from the love and prayers of each other.

N has fallen asleep in the peace of Christ.
As we leave his/her body here, we entrust *him/her*,
with faith and hope in everlasting life,
to the love and mercy of our Father
and surround *him/her* with our love and prayer.

(p. 246)

A Funeral Vigil

Note

What is offered by way of provision for a funeral vigil is helpful and flexible. It can be easily adapted to suit a particular occasion and person.

A vigil need not take place in church, or even in the presence of the coffin. It could be, for example, that the most appropriate place for the vigil is at home. If the vigil is to be kept at home, then a lay minister known to the deceased and the family might take responsibility for leading the prayers. *Common Worship* gives a structure for the vigil, but there may be circumstances when a family member or friend, possibly with the minister's assistance, might co-ordinate something less formal (See Chapter7). The reception of the coffin at church may be followed by a longer vigil of prayer and worship, either immediately or a little later.

The Gathering

Whether formal or informal, the vigil of prayer will need a beginning and an end as well as a middle. The gathering prayers are full of Easter resonance, suggesting, for example, that candles might be lit as a sign of

> . . . the light of Christ, rising in glory,
> banish[ing] all darkness from our hearts and minds.
>
> (p. 247)

Themes

The readings and prayers for the vigil are grouped round various themes. It is suggested that one of the given themes (listed below), or a selection of themes, might be used:

Assurance and Comfort

The Faithfulness of God

The Hope of Heaven

Easter

Advent

An Unexpected Death

A Child

All the material under the thematic headings is imaginative and helpful. Pre-use preparation is necessary; this is not a service that can be used 'straight from the book'. The detail of the Scripture verses used, for example, may benefit from some minor changes to reflect the circumstances of the individual's life and death. When a lay person is leading a time of informal vigil at home, they may find it helpful to discuss the contents of the vigil first with a minister, who should be able to provide the necessary resources. (Where full texts – of Scripture, canticle, prayer, etc. – are not given, they will need to be accessed from elsewhere.)

The themes provide for a variety of situations. Appropriate response can therefore be made for pastoral need and the circumstances of the death, as well as for the time of year. For most families, and for prayers at home, one theme will probably provide enough material. There is quite a weight of Scripture. If a vigil service was to be held in church, perhaps involving a range of people from the church and community, as well as from the family, it would be good to include some symbolic actions, like the candle lighting, some times of silence and some singing. Suitably chosen hymns or songs might replace the canticle. One or two short spiritual but non-biblical readings might be included. The prayer at the end of each section need not be a set prayer, but might be a little more extended and personal.

Ending
The vigil concludes with the Lord's Prayer and an ending prayer.

On the Morning of the Funeral

Note
This is another short act of worship that could be led by a friend or family member. Helpfully, a full text is given. The prayers give the opportunity for a few moments of recollection and prayer before setting out for the Funeral.

Preparation
The bidding is inspired by the imagery of Christ 'who has gone this way before us'.

> As we set out on our journey today,
> we pray for the presence of Christ,
> who has gone this way before us.
>
> *(p. 253)*

The Word

The suggested verses from the Book of Lamentations are very appropriate ones for the time immediately after a death. (Traditionally, the Church has understood these verses as foreshadowing the death and burial of Christ; they are used, for example, in some of the services on Holy Saturday.)

Prayer

There is just one prayer; it is strongly affirmative and encouraging. The first half is particularly powerful:

Heavenly Father,
you have not made us for darkness and death,
but for life with you for ever.
Without you we have nothing to hope for;
with you we have nothing to fear . . .

(p. 254)

The Outline Order for the Funeral of a Child

Instead of a full service order for the Funeral of a child, there are two outline service orders, derived from the authorized Funeral Service, and the Funeral Service within a Celebration of Holy Communion. The outline orders are supported by a collection of helpful and imaginative resources and suggestions that will enable ministers to respond sensitively and appropriately to the distinctive emotions aroused by the death of a child. The selection of resources addresses different occasions and different ages.

If the Funeral is celebrated in the context of Holy Communion, the service is structured in the same way as is the authorized Funeral Service within a Celebration of Holy Communion.

The Outline Order for the Funeral of a Child

The Gathering

1   The coffin may be received at the door by the minister, or it may be in place before the congregation assembles.

2   Sentences of Scripture may be used.

3   The minister welcomes the people and introduces the service.

4   A tribute or tributes may be made.

5   Authorized Prayers of Penitence may be used.

6   The Collect may be said here or in the Prayers.

Readings and Sermon

7   One or more readings from the Bible. Psalms or hymns may follow the readings.

8   A sermon is preached.

Prayers

9   The prayers usually follow this sequence:

- Thanksgiving for the child's life, however brief
- Prayer for those who mourn
- Prayers of Penitence (if not already used)
- Prayer for readiness to live in the light of eternity

Commendation and Farewell

10 The child is commended to God using authorized words.

The Committal

11 The child's body is committed to its resting place using authorized words.

The Dismissal

12 The service may end with a blessing.

(p. 297)

Resources for the Funeral of a Child

The texts have been carefully crafted so as to be appropriate for a variety of circumstances. They all have a simple dignity. Gentle and loving images and language are used. They are, of course, suggested resources, and their inclusion does not preclude the minister from using his or her own words or other appropriate resources.

The Gathering

There is a greeting and two good simple introductory texts from which to choose.

The first text is particularly appropriate for a baby or young child. The second text is more suited for the Funeral of an older child. The words in brackets in the first text particularly address the needs of parents who might be coping with feelings of fear, bitterness or guilt.

> [We meet in the faith that death is not the end,
> and may be faced without fear,
> bitterness or guilt.]
>
> *(p. 301)*

The texts are warm and encouraging as well as realistic about the emotions within the congregation and factual about what is to be done in the service.

Five sentences are suggested, three of which are special to these circumstances.

> I will comfort you, says the Lord, as a mother comforts her child, and you shall be comforted.
>
> *Isaiah 66.13 (p. 302)*

There is a choice from three opening prayers. The second picks up the imagery of God the parent comforting his children.

> O God, who brought us to birth,
> and in whose arms we die,
> in our grief and shock,
> contain and comfort us;
> embrace us with your love,
> give us hope in our confusion,
> and grace to let go into new life.
>
> *(p. 302)*

Readings

Various Bible text references are given (listed below). All are relatively short. Some have special circumstances in mind.

Psalm 23; Psalm 84.1-4; Song of Solomon 2.10-13; Isaiah 49.15,16; Jeremiah 1.4-8; 31.15-17; Matthew 18.1-5, 10; Mark 10.13-16; John 6.37-40; John 10.27,28; Romans 8.18, 28,35,37-39; 1 Corinthians 13.1-13; Ephesians 3.14-19

Prayers

A prayer structure is suggested:

- Thanksgiving for the child's life, however brief;

- Prayer for those who mourn;

- Prayers of Penitence (if not already used);

- Prayer for readiness to live in the light of eternity.

A large selection (23) of good prayers follows. All the prayers respond to the particular feelings of grief suffered by parents and families where children have died. They give plenty of choice, particularly for Funerals of babies and very young children.

The vast majority of the prayers are for the support of those who mourn. Two or three of these contain an element of thanksgiving for the child's life.

God of all grace and comfort,
we thank you for N ,
and for the place *he/she* held in all our hearts.
We thank you
for the love in which *he/she* was conceived
and for the care with which *he/she* was surrounded.
As we remember times of tears and laughter,
we thank you for the love we shared because of *him/her*,
reflecting that love which you poured upon us
in your Son Jesus Christ our Lord.

(p. 307)

While none of the prayers in this section exclusively prays for the readiness to live in the light of eternity, there are among the general collection of prayers and resources for Funerals plenty of other prayers that do address this.

A small number of the prayers could be used to respond to the death of an older child – possibly of primary school age. (There are more in the general Resources and Prayers section.) Some of these could prove helpful for a minister or teacher to use with other children, say in a school assembly, when mourning the loss of a classmate.

Father, the death of N brings an emptiness into our lives.
We are separated from *him/her*
and feel broken and bewildered.
Give us confidence that *he/she* is safe
and *his/her* life complete with you,
and bring us together at the last
to the wholeness and fullness of your presence in heaven,
where your saints and angels enjoy you
 for ever and ever.

(p. 305)

Another prayer could, with explanation, be adapted and used as a responsive litany with siblings or school friends. It begins

> When we are weary and in need of strength,
> when we are lost and sick at heart,
> we remember N.
>
> When we have a joy we long to share,
> when we have decisions that are hard to make,
> we remember *him/her*.
>
> *(p. 311)*

A larger number of the prayers are particularly appropriate for Funerals of very young babies, including those who are stillborn or who have died unbaptized.

> Heavenly Father, N and N have named their baby N
> – a name to be treasured for ever in their hearts.
> But it was you who formed *him/her* in the womb;
> you knew *him/her* by name before time began.
> Now we commit N into your ever-caring and gentle love;
> *he/she* brought the promise of joy
> to many lives for so short a time;
> enfold *him/her* now in eternal life,
>
> *(p. 311)*

Some of the prayers could help counter misunderstandings about God.

> O God, you do not willingly grieve or afflict your children.
> Look with pity on the suffering of this family in their loss.
> Sustain them in their anguish;
> and into the darkness of their grief
> bring the light of your love.
>
> *(p. 306)*

There is a prayer for other children in the family.

> Lord Jesus,
> we ask you to be close to the children of this family,
> whose lives have been changed by sorrow.
> Give them courage to face their loss,
> and comfort them with your unchanging love.
>
> *(p. 311)*

Prayers of Commendation and Farewell

Six appropriate prayers are given: a general one; a prayer for an older child; a prayer for a young child; a prayer for a baby; a prayer for a stillbirth; a prayer for a miscarriage.

> To you, gentle Father,
> we humbly entrust this child so precious in your sight.
> Take *him/her* into your arms
> and welcome *him/her* into your presence
> where there is no sorrow nor pain,
> but the fullness of peace and joy with you . . .
>
> *(especially suitable for a baby, p. 313)*

The Committal

The forms of committal come from the authorized Funeral Service, and are appropriate for either burial or cremation.

The Dismissal

Four prayers are given, the last of which is personal, and more special to this service.

> May the love of God and the peace of the Lord Jesus Christ
> bless and console you,
> and all who have known and loved N,
> this day and for evermore.
>
> *(p. 315)*

Notes

The notes for the authorized Funeral Service also apply to the

Funeral service for a child, as indicated in the Notes preceding the 'Resources for the Funeral of a Child' section.

Ministers are encouraged to welcome young children to a child's Funeral and to keep their needs in mind in the planning of the service. The importance of using the child's name throughout the service is stressed.

Advice is also given as to the role of the president and the balance of the service.

Theological Note on the Funeral for a Child Dying near the Time of Birth

The theological note particularly addresses the special situation relating to the Funeral Service for a stillborn child.

After the Funeral

At Home after the Funeral

One of the immediate difficulties faced by the bereaved after the death of someone with whom they have shared a home, is going back home after the Funeral. The very emptiness of the house focuses the future loneliness of life without the deceased. This little service, which may be adapted to suit the circumstances, attempts to respond spiritually to that need. A friend, family member, or a representative of the church's pastoral ministry may lead it.

- At the Door

The prayer at the door is a prayer for peace, comfort and light.

The peace of God our heavenly Father,
of Jesus Christ the source of peace,
and of the Holy Spirit the comforter
come upon this house and all who live here.

Open, O God, the door of this house;
let your light shine here to drive away all darkness;
through Jesus Christ our Lord.

(p. 318)

93

● The Word of God

The full text of several short readings is given. These all address the fears and the sense of emptiness that bereaved people may feel as they adjust to a new life without their loved ones.

● Prayers

Just one prayer is given, but the minister or leader is referred to the section 'Resources and Prayers' and encouraged to select appropriate texts. Ministers and lay people exercising this ministry will also have their own favourite prayers and resources, and may in any case prefer to offer prayer more informally.

If the service is used in its entirety, with all the readings, and all in the one place, it could seem overly cerebral and stodgy. The minister might consider going with the bereaved to various rooms in the house and garden (as, say, in a house blessing service) and reading a text or saying a different prayer in each place. Members of the family, including children, could help with the readings. Short additional prayers might need to be found, or written. Symbolic actions, such as lighting a candle, using water or oil in some way, or breaking bread, could be linked with some of the prayers.

The prayer that is given would be good to use as a Grace over food, possibly when everyone comes back to the house after the Funeral. The words of the prayer also serve as a sort of redemptive 'blessing' on a place whose emptiness symbolizes loss.

> Almighty God, the Father of our Lord Jesus Christ,
> whose disciples recognized him as he broke bread
>   at their table after the resurrection:
> we thank you for your strength upholding us
>   in what we have done today,
> and now we ask for your presence to be recognized in this
>   home;
> bring your peace and joy to each place which stirs the
>   memory;
> give your strength and presence in those daily tasks
>   which used to be shared,
> and in all the changes of life give us grace
>   to do your will day by day,
>
> *(p. 321)*

● Conclusion

Verses from Psalm 121 may be used, though these are additional Bible verses in a service already heavy with Scripture, but the familiar words of an Old Testament blessing are very appropriate:

> The Lord shall keep you from all evil;
> it is he who shall keep your soul.
> The Lord shall keep watch over your going out
>   and your coming in,
> from this time forth for evermore.
>
> *(p. 322)*

Memorial Service

Memorial or thanksgiving services for those who have died are now more prevalent than they used to be. The provision of a Memorial Service, therefore, is particularly helpful. An outline order is given for use in church several weeks after the Funeral and a Sample Service follows. Some might question the exclusive use of the phrase 'Memorial' Service; the concept of a 'Thanksgiving' Service for a loved person and for a life well lived is also popular and often seen to be more appropriate.

An Outline Order for a Memorial Service

There is a great advantage in being given an outline order for something as personal as a memorial (or thanksgiving) service. Two orders are given, the second of which provides for a Memorial Service within a Celebration of Holy Communion.

The orders are comprehensive and helpfully laid out. No specific mention is made of the Lord's Prayer in the first outline, but it is suggested elsewhere that this would customarily follow the Commendation. When creating a service from the outline order, it might be helpful to consult both the outline and the sample service as they complement each other.

An Outline Order for a Memorial Service

The Gathering

1   The minister welcomes the people and introduces the service.

2   Sentences of Scripture may be used.

3   Authorized Prayers of Penitence may be used.

4   The Collect may be said here or in the Prayers.

Readings and Sermon

5   One or more readings from the Bible.
    Psalms or hymns may follow the readings.

6   Other songs and readings may be used and a tribute or tributes made.

7   A sermon is preached, testimony may be given and an authorized Creed or Affirmation of Faith may be used.

Prayers

8   The prayers usually follow this sequence:

   * Thanksgiving for the life of the departed

   * Prayer for those who mourn

   * Prayers of Penitence (if not already used)

   * Prayer for readiness to live in the light of eternity.

Commendation and Dismissal

9   The dead person is commended to God with authorized words.

10 The service may end with a blessing.

(p. 331)

If there is a Liturgy of the Sacrament, it precedes the Commendation and continues with the Peace. Any of the authorized eucharistic prayers may be used.

Memorial Service: A Sample Service

The sample service is particularly helpful in that it gives some ideas as to both content and shape. Some appropriate texts and prayers are suggested by way of example. The rubrics give ideas as to the construction of the service, indicating, for example, where tributes might be placed and where the hymns might go.

The following is a simple summary of the contents of the sample service. The headings and the order of events in the outline service are not identical to the headings and order of events in the sample service, and that is an encouragement to use these provisions flexibly. Optional prayers etc. in the sample service are bracketed.

The Gathering

Welcome/greeting and introduction; (sentences, hymn); Opening Prayer

Readings and Sermon

(Canticle, with response); New Testament reading; sermon; (sharing of memories; tributes, songs or readings; thanksgiving prayer in response to memories/tributes); short authorized affirmation of faith

Prayers

Prayers of Penitence and Absolution; Prayers of Intercession; (hymns may be sung and testimony given); Prayers of Thanksgiving

Commendation and Dismissal

Commendation; the Lord's Prayer; the Peace (not shared)

Conclusion

Biblical sentence; final prayer and blessing

The sample Memorial Service includes several interesting features. It flows from the perception of the individual as human, frail and sinful, into the Christian understanding of men and women transformed by God into the full glory of his children.

The remembering of the dead person and the thanksgiving for their life is set alongside the Scripture readings. The prayer after the sermon acknowledges that the lives of Christian individuals reveal aspects of the nature of God.

> We bless you that in bearing your image
> *he/she* has brought light to our lives;
> for we have seen
>   in *his/her* friendship reflections of your compassion,
>   in *his/her* integrity demonstrations of your goodness,
>   in *his/her* faithfulness glimpses of your eternal love.
>
> *(p. 337)*

The credal statement that follows leads into an acknowledgement of human sinfulness and therefore prayers of penitence. Then the prayers of intercession, thanksgiving and commendation lead naturally into the reassurance and affirmation of Christ's Peace, which makes possible and proclaims the transformation of the individual into the likeness of God himself.

> . . . as we believe your power to have raised
>   our Lord Jesus Christ from the dead,
> so may we trust your love to give eternal life to all
>   who believe in him.
>
> *(p. 344)*

Notes

The notes that precede the Sample Service suggest that if the Memorial Service takes place on the same day as, or very soon after, the Funeral, the Funeral Service should be used, without the Committal. Thought needs to be given as to whose needs the Memorial (or Thanksgiving) Service should be meeting, and how that might be done. In some circumstances, for example, where

Funeral and memorial services are held fairly close together, the minister and family may feel that a complete duplication of the Funeral Service would not help the bereaved family move on through the grief process. They might therefore prefer the service to be more a mixture of Funeral service and memorial service.

It should be clear throughout the service who is the president. The central focus on the Word of God, prayer and thanksgiving is seen to be important, and the inclusion of other speakers, as well as of music and non-biblical readings, should not unbalance the service from that central focus.

The order for the Memorial Service given in the *Common Worship* Pastoral Services is appropriate only for a service for a single individual and for the weeks after the Funeral. It is not an appropriate service for annual memorial services, such as on All Souls' Day. For these regular services, provision is made in *The Promise of his Glory* and the forthcoming *Common Worship* Times and Seasons volume.

Prayers for use with the Dying and at Funeral and Memorial Services

The prayers are ordered sequentially, providing resources from the time of death to the gathering for the Funeral.

Those looking for prayers for the faithful departed will find a small number of suitable prayers among the authorized Prayers of Entrusting and Commending.

Prayers

Prayers with dying people

Four prayers are given; the first three will be familiar to many: 'Soul of Christ, sanctify me'; 'Christ be with me, Christ within me'; 'Lord Jesus Christ, we thank you for all the benefits you have won for us'. Each of these prayers, if known by the dying person, would be good to say at the bedside, since they would be able to participate.

The third prayer, best known in the first person plural, could be expressed in the first person singular.

> Lord Jesus Christ, [I] thank you
> for all the benefits you have won for [me] . . .
>
> *(p. 346)*

The fourth prayer is striking. It is a 'new' prayer for a dying person and for those who love them and watch with them. It might be best prayed outside the room with the relatives. It could also be a very helpful prayer for people to use in quite a different context: when loved ones are suffering from dementia.

> Lord,
> in weakness or in strength
> we bear your image.
> We pray for those we love
> who now live in a land of shadows,
> where the light of memory is dimmed,
> where the familiar lies unknown,
> where the beloved become as strangers.
> Hold them in your everlasting arms,
> and grant to those who care
>   a strength to serve,
>   a patience to persevere,
>   a love to last,
>   and a peace that passes human understanding.
> Hold us in your everlasting arms,
> today and for all eternity;
> through Jesus Christ our Lord.
>
> *(p. 347)*

Gathering Prayers

Three alternative gathering prayers are given, all of which address the anguish of grief.

Kyries and Prayers of Penitence

This traditional way of praying for the mercy of God is another illustration of the way the Church has used sentences of Scripture in worship.

Four scriptural kyries are given here, with the texts coming mainly from the Psalms.

There are various points in our worship at the time of death at which prayers of penitence are appropriate. Any of these kyries, with or without the responses, could be helpfully said with someone who is dying. They would be equally suitable during a Funeral Vigil, in the Funeral Service and in a Memorial Service. In some circumstances, the kyries can be seen as gentler ways of encouraging penitence than the more focused prayers of confession.

Collects

These are the alternative collects for the Funeral Service. They are among the small number of prayers that refer to our future hopes for the faithful departed.

Thanksgiving for the Life of the Departed

The main bulk of the prayers in this resource collection addresses the headings listed in the rubric which relate to the prayers in the Funeral service.

- Thanksgiving for the life of the departed;
- Prayer for those who mourn;
- Prayers of penitence (if not already used);
- Prayer for readiness to live in the light of eternity.

Ten prayers of thanksgiving are given. Each prayer has its own particular nuance, but the differences between them are not great.

Prayers for Those who Mourn

Some twenty-three prayers are given for those who mourn. There are many helpful prayers among them, all showing sensitivity to the various stages and feelings of grief: sorrow, anguish, regret, failure, guilt, fear, shock, hurt, anger, brokenness, emptiness, tears, loneliness, weariness, and so on. The wide variety of prayers enables us to respond to the many different situations from which people grieve.

Some of the prayers are appropriate for those who mourn the death of children, young people, younger and middle-aged adults, husbands and wives, parents and others. Other prayers could be used after a long illness, a sudden or violent death, or after a suicide. (See also Resources for the Funeral of a Child).

The two prayers after a suicide are particularly important, and relate to a situation where it can be difficult to find the right words. The first prayer refers to the person who has died, the second is a more general prayer for all those who are despairing and depressed.

> Eternal God and Father,
> look in mercy on those who remember *N* before you.
> Let not the manner of *his/her* death
> cloud the good memories of *his/her* life.
> For *N* the trials of this world are over
> and death is past.
> Accept from us all that we feel
> even when words fail;
> deliver us from despair
> and give us strength to meet the days to come . . .
>
> *(p. 360)*

Prayers for Readiness to live in the Light of Eternity

There are some old favourites among these prayers, as well as some newer ones. Among the newer prayers, some use mainly traditional biblical imagery and phrases, others address our sinfulness and our fear of death, and one or two use pictorial and psychological imagery in original new ways.

Some prayers have seasonal overtones. This prayer, for example, might be appropriate for a Funeral during Christmas-tide.

> Living God,
> you have lit the day with the sun's light
> and the midnight with shining stars.
> Lighten our hearts with the bright beams
> of the Sun of Righteousness

> risen with healing in his wings,
> Jesus Christ our Lord.
> And so preserve us in the doing of your will,
> that at the last we may shine
> as the stars for ever . . .
>
> *(p. 364)*

Litanies and Responsive prayers

Seven forms are given. The selection of prayers reveals a gentle sensitivity to the theological niceties of a variety of Christian traditions.

Several of these responsive forms would fit in particularly well for the intercessions at a Funeral set in the context of a Holy Communion service. The congregation at such a service might well be more confident in the expression of Christian faith, and thus more at ease with prayers that are expressive of resurrection assurance and hope. For those whose instinct is to offer prayers for the faithful departed, there are some useful options in this section.

Two of the prayers could be used at the Funeral of a child or young person. One of these, with its response 'Bless us and keep us, O Lord', would be good to use with a group of children mourning the loss of one of their friends.

Prayers of Entrusting and Commending – see page 58

Blessings and other Endings

The prayer resources conclude with a small collection of blessings and ending prayers. These address the many and various circumstances of Funeral ministry. We are given, for example, the opportunity to pick up biblical imagery that may have been used in earlier prayers.

> May Christ the good Shepherd
> enfold *you* with love,
> fill *you* with peace,
> and lead *you* in hope,
> to the end of *your* days;
> and the blessing . . .
>
> *(p. 378)*

Prayers for use after Psalms

Ten prayers are given in this section, which may be said immediately after the psalm selected for the service.

Bible Readings and Psalms for use at Funeral and Memorial Services

Eight New Testament readings are printed in full.
A good selection of references is given for readings from the Old Testament and Apocrypha, Psalms, New Testament and Gospel. Other suitable biblical readings may be used. The rubric indicates that any suitable translation of the Bible may be used.

A rich resource

Never before has the Church of England put such a pastorally helpful collection of services, prayers and resources into the hands of its ministers. Within the covers of the one book, *Pastoral Services*, we now have ample spiritual resources to assist liturgical and pastoral ministry both with those who are dying and also amongst those who are bereaved. The challenge now both to ordained and lay ministers of the Church, is how they might make the best possible use of this rich resource.

The following three chapters explore some of the ways in which the new resources may be used: in ministry before death, at the time of the Funeral, and amongst the bereaved.

PART 3

Making the services work for us

4 Preparing for death

> Two years ago I found myself having to speak at the funeral of a 16-year-old girl who died in our Yorkshire dale. I said stumblingly that God was to be found in the cancer as much as in the sunset. That I firmly believed, but it was an intellectual statement. Now I have to ask if I can say it of myself, which is a much greater test.
>
> *John Robinson, Sermon: 'Learning from Cancer',*
> *23 October 1983*

Death in perspective

In 1983, Bishop John Robinson's doctor told him that he had cancer of the pancreas and only six months left to live. In 1963, when he was Bishop of Woolwich, Robinson had written a best-selling book, *Honest to God*, in which he challenged the ways in which many people thought about God. Could that same honesty about God support him twenty years later when he faced the ultimate challenge of death?

At the time of the diagnosis, Robinson was living in Cambridge. He was popular and highly thought of. The fact of his illness affected everyone who knew him. In October 1983 he preached a sermon about 'finding God in the cancer'. That sermon had tremendous repercussions, and must have been about the most photocopied sermon of the day. His words inspired many people, most especially families knowing someone who, like Robinson, was living with cancer. *Why?*

Two things in particular seem to have struck home. First, there was that shocking yet exhilarating phrase he had used two years previously: 'God is in the cancer as much as in the sunset.' That was so different from current attitudes. And secondly, there was Robinson's personal courage as he worked out his self-confessed 'intellectual' statement in his personal experience. He was honest; he told people how it really was for him: shock, the temptation to cancel everything, and then a turning point. Robinson came to see that the way forward for him was to learn to live more urgently: 'giving the most to life and getting the most from it, while it is on offer.'

> Christians above all are those who should be able to bear reality and show others how to bear it.
>
> *John Robinson, 'Learning from Cancer'*

Always famous for being 'honest to God', Robinson became equally famous for showing Christians how to face death. In the way he approached his own death, he exercised a very real and personal ministry to his fellow Christians as they came to face theirs.

Preparing for eternal life

> 'Preparing for death' is not the otherworldly pious exercise stamped upon our minds by Victorian sentimentality, turning away from the things of earth for the things of 'heaven'. Rather, for the Christian, it is preparing for 'eternal life', which means real living, more abundant life, which is begun, continued, though not ended, now.
>
> *John Robinson, 'Learning from Cancer'*

The Church has always seen ministry at the time of death as a priority of pastoral care. All Christians have to learn how to die, and their Christian faith, the primary context for that learning, is always lived out in the ever-changing context of their times. Christianity is a faith 'for now' as well as a faith 'for us'. God is ever to be encountered and loved 'in the present moment', whatever that present moment may hold.

For John Robinson, that understanding meant living each moment of life fully, even those moments of his life when he was full of cancer. Each and every moment was a moment of opportunity for preparation for eternal life.

> God is to be found in the cancer as in everything else. If he is not, then he is not the God of the Psalmist who said, 'If I go down to hell, thou art there also', let alone of the Christian who knows God most deeply in the Cross. And I have discovered this experience to be one full of grace and truth.
>
> *John Robinson, 'Learning from Cancer'*

Ministry at the Time of Death

> An apocryphal story is told of a residential meeting of the House of Bishops. During a social time, one of the bishops suddenly and unexpectedly collapsed. The Archbishop of Canterbury rushed to his side. He muttered something. 'He wants to be anointed,' said the Archbishop, turning to his Chaplain, 'Get me an ASB.' 'There is no order for anointing in the ASB, Your Grace,' said the Chaplain. The sick bishop spoke again. 'He wants me to hear his confession,' said the Archbishop, 'Pass me an ASB.' 'There is no order for confession in the ASB, Your Grace,' said the Chaplain. The bishop breathed his last. 'He's dead,' said the Archbishop. 'There is a funeral service,' said the Chaplain.
>
> *Martin Dudley (ed.)*, A Manual for Ministry to the Sick, SPCK, 1997

The prayers for the dying and for those who support them communicate the faith of the Church in the presence of death. A major difference between the Funeral Service and the prayers for the dying, however, is that while the Funeral Service is intended for all who request it, the prayers before death are in the main used with people who are practising Christians. That does not, however, preclude the ministers of the Church from using these prayers as they respond to the pastoral needs of anyone who turns to the Church for support when they are dying.

Death is the earthly climax of a dying person's life of Christian discipleship. In her liturgical ministry with the dying, the Church offers worship and prayer to encourage and support Christians who are on the last stages of the journey towards the ultimate vision of 'God with us'.

Each individual is at a different stage in the journey of faith, not least when they come to die. But nobody except God knows the point each person has reached. The liturgy, therefore, does not differentiate between people, and the liturgical minister makes no presumptions. All Christians are on the same journey, and in the same need of 'grace and truth'.

Common Worship – stages of preparation for death

> The true Christian is ever dying while he lives; he is on his bier, and the prayers for the sick are saying over him [*sic*]. He has no work but that of making his peace with God, and preparing for the judgement. He has no aim but that of being found worthy to escape the things that shall come to pass and to stand before the Son of Man. And therefore day by day he unlearns the love of this world, and the desire of its praise; he can bear to belong to the nameless family of God, and to seem to the world strange in it, and out of place, for so he is.
>
> And when Christ comes at last, blessed indeed will be his lot. He has joined himself from the first to the conquering side; he has risked the present against the future, preferring the chance of eternity to the certainty of time; and then his reward will be but beginning, when that of the children of this world is come to an end.
>
> *J. H. Newman,* The Spear of Gold: Revelations of the Mystics, *(edited by H. A. Reinhold), Burns Oates, 1947*

Common Worship identifies four stages in the Christian's final preparation for death: Reconciliation, the Laying on of Hands and Anointing, Holy Communion and Commendation ('Ministry at the Time of Death'). Each stage is supported by the Word of God and by prayer. Undergirding these final stages of preparation there has been a Christian lifetime of preparation. When death comes, however, spiritual needs are focused, and are unique to each individual.

How can we use the new *Common Worship* provisions to help ourselves and each other, as unique individuals, die?

Ministry at the Time of Death: Using the texts

Preparation

For those who are dying from a terminal illness, there are extended periods during the final days and hours when they are asleep or unconscious. There are phrases here that can be repeated aloud at the bedside during these silent hours. These short texts are scriptural prayers that can be said by family and friends as well as by a minister; they can also be helpful to those who watch during the difficult hours of waiting.

> 'I sat by Joan's bedside, and I didn't know what to do. I felt speechless. I needed some words to link the gap between us.'
>
> *A husband in the hospice, watching beside his unconscious wife.*

Short scriptural texts can be accessed from memory. They are therefore good prayers and affirmations of faith in emergencies, which is an important factor in ministry to someone dying, for example, as a result of an accident.

Although these short scriptural texts are most likely to be used when death is imminent, some would be helpful 'arrow' prayers for any time after the first diagnosis of, say, terminal illness, either by the person facing the illness, or by their friends and family. A single-sentence prayer can be directed to God at, for example, a moment of panic or pain; or said over and over again in private prayer by someone coming to terms with their illness:

> The Lord is my light and my salvation; whom then shall I fear?
>
> Psalm 27.1

Good 'arrow' prayers help us focus on God at the difficult times of pain and fear, and a minister could add to this collection. There are many other scriptural phrases that may address an individual's particular need.

> When Joanna knew that her cancer had not been cured by chemotherapy she was afraid. An important aspect of the ministry of the Church to her and to her family was to pray that she might experience the love of God ministering to her in her fear. Short prayers that she could repeat over and over again helped her discover that 'love conquers fear'. That discovery was a turning point for her and her family.
>
> There is no fear in love, but perfect love casts out fear (1 John 4.18).

In the case of 'we' sentences, it might sometimes be more helpful to individualize the prayers and say 'I' instead of 'we'.

Preparation: opportunities for ministry

On first hearing that an illness is terminal

> *Whether we live, or whether we die, we are the Lord's.*
> *We will be with the Lord for ever.*
> *We will see God as he is.*

When feeling afraid

> *The Lord is my light and my salvation, whom then shall I fear?*
> *Be strong . . . he shall comfort your heart; wait patiently for*
>   *the Lord!*

When feeling inadequate and unprepared

> *To you, O Lord, I lift up my soul.*
> *The steadfast love of the Lord never ceases.*
> *In my Father's house there are many dwelling places.*

112

At times of doubt

I believe that I shall see the goodness of the Lord.
You have redeemed me, O Lord, faithful God.

When in pain

Who will separate us from the love of Christ?
My soul is athirst for God, even for the living God.

When death is near

Into your hands I commend my spirit.
Come, you that are blessed of my Father; inherit the kingdom
*   prepared for you.*
Today you will be with me in paradise.

Reconciliation

Most members of the Church of England confess their sins to
God in their private prayers and through a prayer of general
confession in church. In the quiet time of recollection before the
general confession, the individual may make a private
acknowledgement to God of specific sins. Some church
members, however, are accustomed to making a personal
confession of their particular sins in the presence of a priest who
will give them absolution. The encouragement to penance
within the 'Ministry at the Time of Death' texts allows for 'some
expression of penitence'. There may be specific sins that an
individual wishes to confess before they die. The Church of
England has always made provision for an individual to make a
special confession of their sins and to receive priestly absolution.
(See the rubrics for the Visitation of the Sick in *The Book of
Common Prayer.*)

The *Common Worship* provision for ministry at the time of death
allows for a minister to 'encourage some expression of penitence'
and offers several prayers of confession, a prayer of priestly
absolution, with an alternative prayer should the minister be a
deacon or lay person.

The ministry of Reconciliation is essentially a private and
personal ministry. If someone has never experienced the spiritual
release that can come from a personal confession in the presence

of a priest, the opportunity to do so can be experienced as a real spiritual gift.

> For some time, Alf's family had been divided. It wasn't entirely Alf's fault, but his unforgiving attitude to one of his children had contributed to the breakdown of relationships. When he was dying, he came to realize that if the relationship with his son was ever to be restored, he had to begin the process of reconciliation there and then. Conversations with his priest led to his making a special private confession. He was strengthened by this experience to write to his son and apologize for what he had done to hurt him, and to ask for his forgiveness. Alf's apology and need brought his son to visit him before he died. The encounter didn't immediately heal all the divisions within the family, but it brought Alf peace of mind, and began a process of reconciliation within the family.

Reconciliation: opportunities for ministry

At any time after having been told that death is inevitable

The individual may want to talk privately to the minister or to make a more formal act of confession in the presence of a priest.

The service of Holy Communion includes prayers of confession and absolution; the ministry of reconciliation may therefore be exercised regularly in the context of that sacrament, whether in church, at home or in hospital.

Texts of confessional prayers may be given to the individual for use in their private prayers. The first of the prayers printed in this section of Common Worship is easily committed to memory:

> Lord Jesus Christ,
> Son of God,
> have mercy on me,
> a sinner.
>
> *(p. 220)*

Near the time of death

Short preparatory texts might be repeated as suggested in the *Common Worship* provision. It is important that people should be helped to be aware that the time of death is approaching. If the dying person is conscious and able to speak, the minister may ask if there are specific things they wish to confess to God. Any of the printed prayers of confession may be used.

The prayer of absolution is addressed to the dying person and may be accompanied by the laying on of hands.

Prayers with dying people

A ministry of prayer surrounds every aspect of the ministry at the time of death. Special prayers are provided in *Common Worship* for use with dying people when death is imminent. One litany is printed in the main text; other prayer suggestions are given in the resource collection of prayers that supports all the pastoral services around death. Prayers said with a dying person are meant to be prayers that they can hear and respond to. They are not private prayers, nor are they prayers of entrusting and commending. And although these prayers may help family and friends, they are not prayers for those who watch with the dying; a minister may make other opportunities for their prayer needs to be addressed.

John spent his last weeks of life in a nursing home. Fiercely independent, he had lived at home for as long as possible. When the minister came to visit him, he would send his (adult) children away so that his priest could say prayers with and for him, and for his family. His children, though, also needed spiritual support. They found it in their home church and in the support of their minister. They were very attached to their father, yet neither of them could cope with the thought of sitting with Dad through to his death; they wanted to remember him as he was in life. He was at peace and ready for death. But they found it difficult to leave him for the last time. The prayers of the church for the dying, said with the minister at John's bedside on their last visit, helped his children feel at peace. They had done what they could for their father, and could leave him in God's safe hands.

Prayers with dying people: opportunities for ministry

We pray for the dying person

The litany printed in the main body of the text enables the dying and those surrounding them to face the reality of the coming death. Although the litany is intended to be said in the presence of the dying person, it is also a good prayer for the family and friends of the dying person to say for him or her wherever they are. The grace prayed for is the mercy of God.

Graciously hear us, Lord Jesus Christ,
that it may please you to deliver your servant N from all evil
    and from eternal death,
hear us, good Lord.
That it may please you mercifully to pardon all N's sins,
hear us, good Lord.
That it may please you to give N peace, rest and gladness,
raising *him/her* to new life in your kingdom,
hear us, good Lord.
That it may please you to bring us, with N and all your saints
to a joyful resurrection,
hear us, good Lord.

(p. 224)

There is a potential for response

There are additional prayers that may be said 'with dying people' in the general prayer resources, but they are not litanies. The first two prayers in that section, however, could be turned into litanies by people repeating the prayer lines after the minister. St Patrick's Breastplate was most probably a Celtic prayer for God's surrounding presence and defence. It is therefore a very appropriate one to say in the presence of death. It could be very powerful used repetitively with the dying person.

Christ be with me, Christ within me,
Christ behind me, Christ before me,
Christ beside me, Christ to win me,
Christ to comfort and restore me.

Christ beneath me, Christ above me,
Christ in quiet, Christ in danger,
Christ in hearts of all that love me,
Christ in mouth of friend and stranger.

(p. 346)

The prayers may also offer support for those who watch with the dying

Sometimes those sitting with a dying loved one who is showing signs of distress need words of prayer that address their situation directly. The fourth of the prayers with dying people may be appropriate.

Lord,
in weakness or in strength
we bear your image.
We pray for those we love [or N]
who now live in a land of shadows,
where the light of memory is dimmed,
where the familiar lies unknown,
where the beloved become as strangers.
Hold them in your everlasting arms,
and grant to those who care
        a strength to serve,
        a patience to persevere,
        a love to last,
        and a peace that passes human understanding.
Hold us in your everlasting arms,
today and for all eternity . . .

(p. 347)

The Laying on of Hands and Anointing

The laying on of hands and anointing are symbolic actions that have been part of the Church's ministry since its earliest days. Seen in the context of Christ's gift of salvation, these signs are not restricted to ministry at the time of death, but are an integral part of the Church's wider provision for ministry to the sick and the troubled. As such, they are at the heart of several of the services in the *Common Worship* provision for wholeness and healing.

The laying on of hands with prayer is an ancient Christian tradition. It symbolizes both blessing and also the invocation of the power and work of God's Holy Spirit. Olive oil has been traditionally valued for its healing powers, hence the Church's practice of anointing with oil as part of her regular healing ministry.

> Barbara was a doctor, and in many ways very much in control of her own dying. She was strong at supporting her two children, both in their early twenties, through the trauma of her death. Her own faith was a tremendous inspiration to them. Barbara came home from hospital for her final few days of life. When she was ready, she asked her children to tell the priest that the time had come for the final prayers. As a doctor, she wanted 'the full rites' of the Church. She was only just conscious when the priest came but was able to raise her own hand to her forehead after the anointing and to say her last word, 'Amen'.

Laying on of hands and anointing: opportunities for ministry

In the regular course of parish worship

Those churches which regularly minister wholeness and healing through the laying on of hands and anointing, will already have given their members an understanding of the grace that is given and received through this ministry. (Such regular ministry can be seen as part of the Church's long-term preparation of Church members for their death.)

At any time after having been told that death is inevitable

The ministry can be exercised both in public worship and also in the less formal surroundings of someone's home. It may sometimes be helpful to involve other members of the church. There are some circumstances, though, when it is more appropriately exercised with the individual alone.

At the time of death

The laying on of hands and anointing are intimately bound up with each other. While this is obviously a ministry to the dying person, it can also strengthen and uphold those watching with them. The minister must exercise sensitivity as to whether or not to ask others to join in the laying on of hands with him or her. If that sharing ministry is something that the dying person welcomed in life, it is more likely to be appropriate at the time of death.

Holy Communion

Regular reception of Holy Communion is an essential part of the pattern of Christian living. Even when someone is reluctant to display any emotion in talking about their illness, their fears or their faith, the quiet celebration of Holy Communion week by week, at church, at home or in hospital, will often give them all the spiritual blessings they need. It is a service in which others can join without things getting too emotional. Another very special thing about the service of Holy Communion for many people is that the sacrament focuses for them the unseen yet real presence with them of those they love who have died.

Mary had known that she had a terminal illness for some years before she died. Her high priority was the weekly Prayer Book Communion service. While she was able, she continued to attend her beloved 8 a.m. service. When weakness prevented her, the priest brought Holy Communion to her. She didn't talk much about her illness, she got on with doing the things that she wanted to complete before she died. At her final Holy Communion service, her daughters were with her. She wasn't conscious and could not therefore receive communion herself. But her daughters did. When Mary's funeral was being planned, her family as well as her church agreed that the funeral must be in the context of the service of Holy Communion. 'That's what she would have wanted.'

Holy Communion: opportunities for ministry

Regularly throughout the Christian life

The Holy Communion service is important for all Christians; it strengthens them in their Christian living, and encourages them when they die. Through its words and actions, Holy Communion speaks of life with God for ever, thus its regular reception forms a life-long preparation for death.

At home

Reception of Holy Communion at home, especially when people are sick or housebound, is an important part of the Church's ministry. The celebration of Holy Communion can be relatively informal, if that is appropriate, and prayers can be offered for the sick person and their family.

In hospital

It is customary for the hospital chaplain rather than the parish minister to bring Holy Communion to patients when they are in hospital. When asked, however, most chaplains are sympathetic should the ill person particularly request the occasional ministry of their own priest.

At the time of death

The dying person may not be able to receive Holy Communion during the last days of their life. The Church has long had a tradition of 'spiritual communion', believing that, in such circumstances, communicants can partake by faith of the body and blood of Christ and of the benefits conveyed in the sacrament. It is very appropriate for other Christians close to the person who is dying to share in their last service of Holy Communion. They might be asked to read a Bible lesson, or to contribute to the prayers.

The Commendation

The Commendation, or prayer of entrusting, is the Church's last word to the dying person. It is not always possible to say the prayer at the precise moment of death. A minister may therefore appropriately use the prayer when the person's death is seen as imminent. While we do not know when someone is no longer able to hear, this prayer is addressed to them, and sends them on their way from this life to the next.

> 'I think he really is going this time.' This was the brief phone message from Tom's daughter to their vicar. 'Can you come?' The vicar, who had anointed Tom on the previous visit, was able to come immediately and say the prayer of commendation with Tom. The prayer used was a traditional one which he would have known. Tom died shortly after the vicar had left.

A life-long ministry

> The time to prepare for Death is at the height of Life, they are both part of the same pilgrimage.
>
> *Gerald Priestland, 'On Death and Dying'*

While *Common Worship* provides for ministry 'at the time of death', one of the most important aspects of the church's pastoral ministry is providing life-long preparation for death. The more conscientiously this task is fulfilled through the regular worship life and education programme of the local church, the more able Christians should be to come to terms with death when they have to. Hopefully, they will also be the more prepared for sudden death, if that is the way they must go.

> 'Preparing for death' is . . . preparing for 'eternal life', which means real living, more abundant life, which is begun, continued, though not ended, now.'
>
> *John Robinson, 'Learning from Cancer'*

The Church's regular ministry of word and sacrament, of reconciliation, wholeness and healing, faithfully exercised week by week, in little ways as well as in larger ways, offers myriad opportunities to help everyone, young and old, fit and less fit, to prepare for death through every moment of their lives. Even services and prayers for reconciliation and healing are not just an expression of some spiritual crisis ministry, exercised by the fit for the unfit; they are all part of the whole spiritual way of life which prepares us all for eternity, and life with God for ever.

How can we help each other prepare for death in the ongoing life of the Church?

- Encourage church members, whatever their age or state, to think about what might be the implications of living each day as if it were their last.

- Develop the church's liturgical ministries of healing, wholeness and reconciliation.

- Use the offices of Compline or Night Prayer as part of the regular pattern of worship.

- Have the courage to talk, preach and teach about death. (Not just with adults, but in confirmation classes, and, if possible, in the schools in the parish. Bereavement studies are now part of the national curriculum.)

- Base teaching material for parish study groups on the *Common Worship* services and prayers.

- Take especial care over preparation for the annual services on Good Friday, Remembrance Sunday and at All Souls' tide. Involve church members in the preparation.

- Encourage church members to share in home communions, pastoral visiting of the dying and bereaved, and in other aspects of the church's ministry around death.

- Suggest church members pre-plan their own Funerals and offer assistance.

- Make sure in all of this that the ministry team leads by example!

5 The Funeral Service

Great expectations

The Funeral Service lies at the heart of the Church's ministry at the time of death. If this service cannot bear the very great expectations of all who look to the Church of England to bury its dead, then the whole package will be found wanting.

The expectations that are laid on the Funeral Service come from many directions. First, the Church of England as a whole expects its formal worship to reflect its identity as an established Church which is both catholic and reformed. Second, the local churches with their clergy and people look for a liturgy that they can host with integrity and pastoral sensitivity in every possible set of circumstances. Third, those bereaved closest to the deceased hope for a service unique and personal to their loved one, which, while recognizably Christian, also honours their own needs and situation. Fourth, at many Funerals or memorial services there is a gathered, sometimes quite far-flung, community of people who have come to honour the life of the departed, to recall their own memories of him or her and to say farewell. Fifth, though perhaps less frequently, the deceased person themselves may have contributed to the planning of their own service as part of their preparation for death. And lastly, Funeral directors too have their own expectations of the Funeral Service as a part of the overall service they offer their clients. Severally, each one of these groups has high expectations; taken together, the challenge to the Church is immense.

There is one major additional expectation from all these communities that the Church of England Funeral Service must bear. How does it serve the requirement of a Funeral service at the crematorium?

The wider Church of England

The Church of England is proverbially broad. Since the
Reformation, her doctrinal umbrella has covered and still works
to hold together a spectrum of sincerely held theological
positions, sometimes difficult to reconcile. In the case of the
Funeral Service, the major differences in perspective relate to our
theologies of death and after-life. This is particularly focused in
the long history of dissent over prayer for the departed. The
Liturgical Commission has worked very hard to hold together
Anglican catholic and reformed positions. If they have succeeded,
the new services could show that, although Anglicans are, in this
respect, still somewhat divided, there has been gentle movement
towards a truly 'common worship' Funeral service.

Anglicans who were doctrinally 'more catholic than reformed'
hoped that *Common Worship* would produce 'richer liturgical
texts conveying our fellowship with the departed, our solidarity
with them in prayer, and our affectionate commending them into
the Father's hands' (Michael Perham, in *Towards Liturgy 2000*,
ed. Michael Perham, SPCK/Alcuin Club, 1989).

Anglicans who were doctrinally 'more reformed than catholic'
required that the new services should not 'undermine our
assurance that God will fulfil his purposes of salvation for all
who have died in Christ and our confidence that the faithful
departed are "in Christ", "with the Lord"' (Christopher
Cocksworth, *Prayer and the Departed*, Grove Books, 1997).

The compromise that has been reached is effectively that the
'standard service' fulfils the doctrinal requirements of the 'more
reformed' Anglican, while the alternative prayers and
supplementary texts include some additional material, the careful
use of which might supply the further doctrinal dimension hoped
for by 'more catholic' Anglicans. Only time will tell whether
everyone feels that the compromise has worked.

The parish church

The primary concern for most local parish churches is probably
less the finer details of doctrinal controversy than having a liturgy
that is better than the one they had before, and one that they can

host with integrity and pastoral sensitivity in every possible set of circumstances.

Ministers, and those who conduct Funeral services with them, will be looking for a flexible order of service suitable for the Funerals of both old and young, of regular church-goers, of people who are more on the fringe of the church and of those whom the minister may not know at all. It must be appropriate for deaths in all sorts of circumstances. It must work well for Funerals in the parish church as a more extended service, and also for services in a crematorium chapel with all the pressures on time that this may bring.

Local ministers have pastoral hearts but busy lives. They will appreciate a service that responds well to the particular pastoral needs of each death, but which also makes links with the care in the community in which lay church members may be involved.

The bereaved closest to the deceased

While most bereaved families will expect the Funeral service to be recognizably 'Church of England', people have increasingly high expectations that each service will be unique and personal to their departed loved one, and also respond to their own particular needs and situation. They will, as much as anything, therefore judge the service according to these criteria.

The gathered community of those attending the Funeral

Similar expectations are held by those who have come from the deceased's various work and friendship networks. They too want to honour the life of the departed, to recall their own memories of him/her and to say farewell. They will expect the service, and the leader of the service, to do this well. This group of people will perhaps be more aware of how well they can hear and see what is going on. Technological advances in other areas of living have raised people's expectations of audibility, visibility and professional presentation, in church as much as anywhere else.

The deceased

> Jennifer Paterson was talking about her Funeral shortly before she died: 'I'll have a ringside seat for the funeral. Brompton Oratory, please. Latin, with the Dies Irae from Verdi's *Requiem*. Oh, and at the end perhaps a good Negro spiritual' Christopher Howse, *Sunday Telegraph*, 11 August 1999.

The person whose Funeral it is may well have indicated to the minister and his or her relations something of what they hope might happen in their service. Sometimes the suggestions are fairly simple – please sing my favourite hymn; sometimes a complete service might have been planned with the minister as part of the preparation for dying.

Some clergy positively encourage members of their congregations to 'think ahead' and fill in a 'my Funeral' planning sheet that can be filed and brought out when necessary. Sheffield Cathedral, for example, promotes this practice, and a specimen of the form is included with their permission in Chapter 7. Canon Jane Sinclair, the Precentor at Sheffield Cathedral explains that

> the person who completes the form does so with or after discussion with their family/friends and their vicar. Copies should be lodged with the next of kin and with the vicar . . . I have found the forms very helpful when preparing funerals for members of the congregation. The key is to use the requests on the form creatively with the relatives of the person who has died. It is important that the dead person's wishes do not attain the status of 'mustery' (hence the proviso on the form . . .).

The Funeral director

The Funeral director, being the first port of call after most deaths, exercises considerable influence on the bereaved as to where the service should take place, who should officiate, how the service is conducted and what it should contain. If the Church wants to retain its major role in the Funeral business, then she must also attend to the expectations of the Funeral directors.

Funeral directors have businesses to run. Time is a major factor, and so is customer satisfaction. If the local church or minister is unhelpful, seems arrogant or does not do a 'good job', then the undertaker may well take 'the business' elsewhere – which serves no one's interest. (Arguably too, parish clergy should be aware of the strains under which Funeral directors work and of their pastoral needs.)

A service at the crematorium

While we, as church people, may not expect a crematorium Funeral service to be as satisfying as a Funeral service held in the local church, we do expect our authorized service to be as good a tool as possible for a Funeral service held at a crematorium. Does the *Common Worship* Funeral service also fulfil these expectations?

Choices

Common Worship or *The Book of Common Prayer?*

From 1 January 2001, there are only three options for Church of England funerals: *Common Worship, Series 1 Burial Services* (authorized until 2005) or *The Book of Common Prayer.* Families have a right to choose which order of service to use. Experience, however, shows that most people take whatever the minister offers, without asking questions. In many parishes where the experimental use of proposed *Common Worship* forms has been permitted, 'Prayer Book' families have expressed a greater affinity with *Common Worship* than with *The Alternative Service Book.*

The *Common Worship* service has been written with all normal scenarios in mind. It works well for both burials and cremations, and for services in church or crematorium. The Prayer Book service, even in its revised form, works best for ceremonies where the deceased is buried in the churchyard of the church where the Funeral service takes place. It is far less effective for cremations.

Burial or cremation?

More people today are cremated than buried. Various factors – economic, sociological, geographic, ecological or family – contribute to this trend.

Cremation is less time-consuming and less expensive than burial. Most people like to be buried 'with the family'. Today this can mean transporting the deceased quite a distance. It is cheaper and more convenient to bring the ashes to a distant burial ground rather than the body. For those of little, if any, faith, a Funeral in a crematorium is often preferable to a Funeral in a church or chapel. Crematoria offer what has been described as 'a minimal fuss, optional religious content and functional one-stop service'.

Current ecological sensitivity means that people are asking more questions about environmentally friendly practice. The amount of available space for burials is diminishing in this country, and many question whether this is the best use of valuable land. The burial of cremated remains takes up less space than the burial of a body. If no markers are used, the site can – in time – be re-used for new interments. The number of natural burial grounds, cemeteries managed along ecologically sound principles, is increasing. Cremation, on the other hand, releases greenhouse gases.

Although the majority of Funerals in England are cremations, some people still prefer interment. Burial works well when a Funeral has taken place in a church where the churchyard is still open for burials: It can feel gentler and less distressing in the case of the death of a child, or of a young adult. Some people too have a fear of cremation.

What about the ashes?

Common Worship provides for both burial and cremation. The burial of ashes is seen as the equivalent of the burial of the body, and would normally be expected to take place as soon as possible after the Funeral service. In some circumstances, it is pastorally more helpful for the cremation to take place first, and for the 'main' service to be held when the ashes are buried. The *Common Worship* provisions also enable this option.

Ashes should be buried in churchyards, not scattered (Canon B 38.4b). (Regulations vary in cemeteries and civic burial grounds.) Most churchyards have 'gardens of remembrance' or special areas where ashes are interred. If there is already a family grave, this may be a possible site for interring the ashes of a close relation.

With or without Holy Communion?

A Funeral Service within a Celebration of Holy Communion is appropriate for those who were committed communicants at their local church. Whether or not Holy Communion should be an integral part of someone's Funeral service will depend upon the judgement of the parish minister and the relatives of the deceased. The recent tradition of the Church of England has to some extent under-played the importance of the Holy Communion service at Funerals, even when the deceased has been a regular communicant. A church and a family for whom the Holy Communion service is an integral part of their lives may sometimes therefore need encouragement to incorporate a celebration of Holy Communion at some point in the Funeral ceremonies.

> 'Last year we went to the Funeral of a priest who had died suddenly. The church was full, with members of his congregation and parish, his family and fellow clergy. The church and the dead priest were of the Anglican Catholic tradition. The vast majority of people there were communicants. There were an awful lot of words, but no Holy Communion Service. A lot of us went away feeling more distressed than when we came.'
> *Comment from a group of clergy after attending a priest's Funeral which was loosely spun around* The Alternative Service Book *Funeral text*

If both the deceased and their family are regular church-goers, then a Funeral service within the context of Holy Communion is a way of affirming the Christian faith of the deceased and his or her part within the life of the Church, whatever the circumstances of the death. Members of the church will want to join with the family in the Funeral Eucharist, giving thanks to God for the life of a fellow Christian, while also offering to God all their feelings of loss, grief, anger, shock and the like.

'It was absolutely right to have a Holy Communion service for my mother', said a parishioner whose mother died at the age of 104. 'She had been a weekly communicant ever since she was confirmed. The Holy Communion service was at the centre of her Christian life. It would have been quite wrong to do anything else.' (The family and the majority of people who attended the service communicated; non-communicants were invited to come to the altar rail for a blessing and most did. It was a real church community celebration for a Christian lady who had 'gone to glory'.)

Another option for a deceased regular communicant might well be to have a Holy Communion service before the Funeral, the coffin having been brought into church earlier. This might be judged to be pastorally more helpful for the family, if not for the congregation, especially if the death is experienced as premature. The parish Holy Communion service in church on the Sunday following the death will need to respond to the shock and grief of the whole congregation. The texts for the Funeral Service within a Celebration of Holy Communion are very appropriate in these circumstances.

The celebration of Holy Communion is what it always is: 'It focuses our attention both on Christ's sacrifice on the cross and on our assurance of the future resurrection, reminding us forcibly of the communion of saints' (*Anglican Worship Today*, ed. C. Buchanan, T. Lloyd, H. Miller, Collins Liturgical Publications, 1980).

These theological priorities are central to the Christian understanding of life in Christ both before and after physical death. Perhaps the question relating to the Funeral of a communicant Christian should be: why should the Funeral not take place in the context of the Holy Communion service?

The personal touch

Words

While the Church of England does have a 'fixed liturgy', that liturgy is not these days so formal that other, more impromptu words may not be spoken within worship. The *Common Worship* Funeral Service offers many opportunities for a lay person's or the minister's own words (e.g. after the Greeting; in a tribute; introducing the Prayers of Penitence; the Sermon; the main body of Prayers). At all these points in the service, words most appropriate to the deceased, the circumstances of the death and the customary style of the church may be used.

Texts

Biblical texts are at the heart of the Funeral Service, and were selected to address the various and complex emotions experienced by those who mourn. It is suggested that two lessons be read, one from the Old or New Testament and one from the Gospels, and that there be a Psalm or hymn in between. A selection of appropriate New Testament and Gospel readings is given in the Resources section. The resources include a table which gives Further Readings and references from the Old Testament, Apocrypha and the Psalms as well as additional New Testament and Gospel references.

The wide variety of Scripture passages sets the proclamation of the resurrection hope firmly in the fragility of our human context. Between them, the readings acknowledge the apparent futility of death, encourage us in a right remembering of the departed, teach us to hope in our future gathering together in God's kingdom, and encourage us to the continuing witness of a Christian life. Not all the texts are easy to understand, which means that those arranging the service will want to ensure that they are read well.

There is also a good selection of prayers, many of which gently reveal the meaning of the symbols and gestures used in the Funeral Service. As ministers try to select the most appropriate texts for the service, it is helpful to be as aware of the theological dimension of our prayers, as of the need to find texts that address particular pastoral circumstances.

> While we rejoiced in the overall feel of the new Funeral
> Service, we had to search for prayers that didn't mention
> grief too much. Having the Funeral in the context of Holy
> Communion helped set the service in the context we
> wanted: thanksgiving for a fulfilled Christian life.
>
> *(Experience of a family for whom grief felt inappropriate.*
> *They wanted to rejoice because their elderly Christian*
> *relative had been waiting a long time to 'go to heaven'.)*

There is a far greater choice of Bible readings and prayers offered
in the *Common Worship* services than in *The Alternative Service
Book* or *The Book of Common Prayer*, and the person leading
the service should be able to find appropriate texts for most
circumstances. Nothing, however, precludes the use of alternative
appropriate Scripture passages, or prayers from other Christian
sources.

Music

Music plays a very important part in many Funeral services,
probably because music expresses the heights and depths of
feelings in ways that words can not. For this reason perhaps the
choice of music can actually make or break a Funeral service.
Few Funerals take place without any music at all, even if it is
only before and after the service. Often, the choice of music for a
Funeral is the area of personal choice that people feel most
confident about.

Both the Funeral Service and the sample Memorial Service
suggest places where a hymn (or psalm) may be sung, though in
fact these may be sung at any suitable point. The Memorial
Service suggests the possibility of 'other songs' at the time of the
Readings and after the Sermon.

The music we choose must allow the expression of the wide
range of emotions felt when someone has died. It must console
the mourners as well as uplift and strengthen them: 'Since music
can evoke strong feelings, the music for the celebration of the
funeral rites should be chosen with great care. The music at
funerals should support, console and uplift the participants and

should help to create in them a spirit of hope in Christ's victory over death and in the Christian's share in that victory' (*Roman Catholic Order of Christian Funerals, 31*).

The appendices and resources to the *Common Worship* material include suggestions for readings, psalms and canticles, though not for suitable hymns or songs. Other publications give helpful lists, though even these are restricted by the compiler's imagination. It is worth photocopying a good list to give to a family who are planning a Funeral, rather than leaving them to rely on their own memories or the Funeral director's suggestions. A parish ministry team might fruitfully compile their own list of possible hymns and songs. It is helpful if the hymns are 'well-known', but there is no need to restrict ourselves to the 'usual' Funeral hymns. We can be more imaginative and inclusive than we often are. Seasonal material, for example, doesn't always come to mind for a Funeral. But why, for example, should a Christmas carol not be included for a Funeral during Christmas-tide?

More and more families want to suggest suitable music for before and after the ceremony. Often the suggestions are of 'secular' music. This can sometimes prove challenging for the church. Some ministers 'solve' the secular music 'problem' by suggesting that this choice be played during the time at the crematorium.

It is perhaps wise not to have a hard and fast rule! A pop song, for example, carefully chosen and consistent with Christian belief, can be both appropriate and intensely moving. At the funeral of the Revd Michael Vasey, a much-loved priest and liturgist, everyone appreciated the inclusion of the song 'Je ne regrette rien'. 'It was wonderful and witty!' people said afterwards.

Service sheets

'I went to a super funeral the other day. It was all in this special service booklet with a glossy cover. Told you where to sit and when to stand – and everything. It was really good. Do you want to see it? There are some nice prayers in it too.'

Service sheets communicate a surprising amount of information. Until recently, they were the sole preserve of the undertaker, and communicated whatever information the undertaker thought was important. (Usually, the words of the hymns, the basic order of events, and instructions about posture.) Often, the service sheet is the only piece of paper to be put into a Funeral congregation's hands.

A church that takes its Funeral ministry seriously will surely want to make sure that the Funeral service sheet enhances the quality of the service itself. Far from being just an instruction sheet, it has the possibility of containing printed prayers and other material that minister to the spiritual needs of the mourners. A carefully planned and well-designed Funeral service sheet should not only help people enter fully into the service, but also give them some spiritual resources for the days and weeks ahead, as they attempt to come to terms with their bereavement.

Given the wide availability of desktop publishing resources, it is now possible to produce very attractively set out printed service sheets at relatively little cost. Parishes that have developed their own professional logos and distinctive styles will want to extend this image to all the services they hold, including Funerals. All the *Common Worship* material is available on disk as well as on the World Wide Web. Perhaps 'information technology friendly' parishes might consider working collaboratively with the local undertakers in order to improve the quality and content of Funeral service sheets.

Symbols

Symbols, signs and gestures are potent attributes of liturgical prayer. The new services indicate a developing understanding within the Church of England of the power of symbols, either to underline or to undermine the worship we offer. In an age of effective visual media, this awareness of the power of visual symbols is particularly important. Are our liturgical signs meaningful and generous in the proclamation of the resurrection, or are they minimal and careless?

In church Funerals, the presence of the congregation is a strong symbolic sign that, as Christians, we live and die, grieve and rejoice, not as lonely individuals, but as members of one fellowship, the body of Christ. This is especially evident when a Holy Communion service is celebrated. The new services promote our awareness of a real sense of Christian fellowship by encouraging greater lay participation in the whole spectrum of services and prayers. In this respect, there can be a very poignant difference between a church Funeral and the Funeral of someone who is outside the local church community. Perhaps ministers using the new services will seize the opportunity to encourage appropriate lay participation in these circumstances too.

The body of the deceased is a natural point of focus for symbolic action and appropriate accompanying prayer. When the coffin is brought into church, it may be sprinkled with water in remembrance of the deceased person's baptism. The minister is encouraged to be generous with this sign of baptismal blessing, and may like to use an evergreen branch possibly taken from the family garden. The minister, or a family member or friend, might cover the coffin with a white pall, a cloth that signifies baptismal life in Christ. Other Christian symbols such as a Bible or a cross, if possible the deceased person's own, may be placed on the coffin. A large lit candle, possibly the Paschal (Easter) Candle, carried by a server or member of the pastoral ministry team, could lead the coffin into church and stand at its head throughout the service, a sign of the presence of the risen Christ.

All these symbolic acts are suggested as possibilities in the *Common Worship* Funeral provisions. Accompanying prayers and sentences are also given which help open up the meaning of the symbols for the mourners. The meaning behind the Christian symbols is unfamiliar to many people today; some will find this unfamiliarity threatening. The Funeral sermon might fruitfully explore one or other of the symbols in its proclamation of the resurrection faith. All this may be new ground for many Anglican congregations, but families and congregations who have experienced this wider use of symbols in Funeral services have welcomed it.

There is also provision within the *Common Worship* Funeral Service for 'suitable symbols' of the life and faith of the departed person to be placed on or near the coffin. Some anxiety has been expressed as to the propriety of this. The 'suitable symbols' are, however, primarily intended to affirm the Christian life and faith of the deceased, and not his or her earthly life and achievements.

The Church of England is perhaps unique in its relation to the crown and the state. In Roman Catholic Funerals, even national flags and the insignia of associations are not supposed to lie on the coffin when it is in church. It is not always easy, in an established church such as our own, to make such a fine distinction between spiritual and earthly symbolism. Our monarchs, for example, are the Supreme Governors of the Church; their coffins, like those of other members of the royal family, are traditionally covered by their personal royal standard. Again, the traditional cover for the coffins of those who have fought for Queen and Country is the Union Flag; and sometimes other insignia, such as hats, are placed on the coffin.

More frequently in a parish, mourners want to place personal gifts of love and farewell on the coffin, such as cards, or the single red rose that is a reminder of the brief flowering of our earthly lives. It is probably wise to be generous in responding to people's grief, but to encourage good practice wherever possible and discourage anything that obviously weakens, trivializes or even undermines the symbolism of Christian faith. In some situations, the alternative of a small table alongside the coffin might be offered on which to place some of these earthly tokens and memorabilia. It might also be appropriate, when the token is personal and from someone very close to the deceased, to suggest that such a token be placed inside the coffin.

Environment

A Funeral celebrated in the local church benefits from being in familiar surroundings. Thought, however, needs to be given to the way in which the building is used for Funerals, and also as to how local church members might share in the 'hosting' of what can be seen to be a 'family' (sometimes a more 'extended family') event. Careful attention to what might seem minor details can make a big difference.

This is a possible checklist:

- Has thought been given as to who is coming and where they should sit?

- Are there welcomers or sidespeople to greet those attending the funeral?

- Who meets the coffin, and will it be 'received' at the church or lich-gate, if there is one, or at the main door? What words should be used?

- If the church has bells, should one be tolled as the procession makes its way from church gate to church door?

- Where and when should the sentences be said?

- Should we begin with the traditional starting sentence, 'I am the resurrection and the life, says the Lord', or reserve that particular sentence until the entrance into church?

- If the reception is at the church gate, perhaps the sprinkling of water could be done at the main entrance.

- Is the way into church clear?

- Will the choir be present and lead the way with the processional cross?

- Should an assistant, server or member of the pastoral team carry the lit (possibly Paschal) candle?

- Where is the best place for the coffin to stand, not just for the sake of the service, but to ensure that at the end of the service it may be lifted and turned with dignity?

- Is the area where the coffin will stand well lit? Might floodlights be used so that the symbols placed on the coffin stand out?

- Who will be placing the Christian symbols on the coffin, and when?

- If a lit candle is used as a symbol of Christ's presence, might the candle be decorated with 'Easter flowers'?

- Should white vestments and furnishings be used to symbolize Easter faith? Or is the Funeral one where the mourners might not understand the colour white, and so might purple or black be better used?

- On the way out, might a muffled peal of bells be appropriate?

These and other practical actions can involve a significant number of members of the church, wardens, sidespeople or welcomers, ringers, servers, choristers, musicians and others.

Their involvement, in often quite simple actions, will focus the love of God and of his Church for the deceased and for those who mourn his or her death.

Special thought needs to be given to what happens in a crematorium, where the 'chapels' are often created as neutral zones in which people of every faith and none can be accommodated. Could we, for the duration of the service, turn a crematorium into a Christian space? Perhaps some church members might accompany the minister and support the mourners. The church's own symbols could be brought and used, a processional cross maybe, lit candles, and a beautifully bound Bible or Gospel book.

Time

> In our secular society the ceremonies that traditionally surrounded death have been gradually eliminated, leaving little to replace them. For most of us there will be no last rites, no final anointing, no confession, no candles, no vigils, no holy oil, no prayers, no masses, no requiems, no wakes, little or no public grieving, and nowadays sometimes not even flowers for the grave . . . We conduct quick, in-out funerals, and believe twenty-minute services . . . 'quite long'. . . When I look for reasons I can find only one. *Because it is too difficult*. The pain just makes it *too* hard.
>
> G. Carey, 'A Death-Denying Circus', from The Penguin Book of Death, *ed. G. Carey and R. Sorenson.*

This is an interesting and challenging quotation (please note however that the author is not George Carey, Archbishop of Canterbury). Do people who take the trouble to come to a Funeral really find even twenty minutes too long? Perhaps it all depends on how the Funeral is conducted. No Christian minister would expect to make the Funeral 'easy', or to take the pain away, but he or she would want to make the best use of the time available.

There are of course real constraints on time created by many of the crematoria time schedules. The twenty-minute slot is proverbial, though it would be interesting to know how accurate the proverb is. It may well be less true today than it used to be.

Some crematoria, for example, are now open on Saturdays; others give forty-five minute slots for all services.

The twenty-minute constraint cannot really enable the best 'send-off' for anyone. Much better, if this is the local crematorium situation, to encourage Funeral directors to suggest church Funerals to their clients as a preferable option. The bare minimum of the *Common Worship* Funeral Service, however, does contain all that is essential and could be contained within twenty minutes, providing there was tight control over the length of the reading, the sermon and the prayers.

- Liturgical greeting, introductory words
- The Collect
- A reading from the New Testament or Gospel
- A Sermon
- Prayers (four subjects suggested – a short form is given)
- The Lord's Prayer
- Commendation
- Set pre-committal text
- Committal
- Ending prayer

This minimum should just be contained in the time available, with dignity and without compromise, and even with some short silences. It might even be possible to include one hymn played at a reasonable speed. (Though the twenty-minute limit probably couldn't stand the strain of a late start should someone else over-run their time allocation!)

Making the most of cremation services

'I was really disappointed. The minister hadn't even taken the trouble to find out that he was always called Harry. Nobody ever called him Wilfred.'

'The funeral was awful. She would have turned in her grave.'

A cremation service can often be the easier, possibly even the cheaper, option for the family, for the Funeral director, and even for a busy minister. It is not easy for a minister to encourage a previously unknown family, with no church links, to have their Funeral service in church. It is even tempting to wonder whether that would be worth his or her time expenditure. The decision in any case has often already been assumed by the Funeral director.

But it is possible, none the less, to deliver a good crematorium service. Virtually every minister would recognize the importance of a pre-Funeral pastoral visit to the family and of knowing something about the person whose Funeral they are taking. In addition, a good relationship between ministers and their local Funeral directors is vital. This is perhaps almost more important in the case of our 'unknown' Funerals than it is for the Funerals of church members. Good working relationships between clergy and the staff at the local crematorium are also important. If all these relationships are positive, then clergy, Funeral directors and crematorium staff can work together to offer a helpful, 'team ministry' Funeral service.

Given all this, Funeral directors should feel more able to trust clergy to assist the family with decisions as to readings, prayers, and even hymns. Service sheets too are better created as a corporate effort between the minister and Funeral director. The staff at the crematorium are usually proud of their building and facilities and, again given a good relationship, will often happily co-operate with those ministers and churches who want to bring and use some of their own symbols.

Individual circumstances

Difficult and apparently meaningless deaths will always test the words of our liturgies. When a child has died, for example, or a young student has committed suicide, so many of the things we usually say about death seem meaningless. We can't talk about natural rhythms of life, because these deaths break the natural rhythms. Neither can we be consoled by a lifetime of achievement: in the case of a child, everything was still hopes and dreams. The Funerals of those who have committed suicide are also pastorally extremely difficult. There are hugely mixed emotions: inability to understand, guilt, fear of judgement, and the need to respond to the dead person's beliefs that they were a failure, or a burden to others.

All Funeral rites exist to give us something to say, and some hope to offer. How can we use the *Common Worship* rites in our attempts to rise to impossible challenges like these?

The death of a child

'One of my first funerals', said a minister, 'was for two stillborn twins. I shall never forget the father and the uncle carrying the two tiny white coffins into the cemetery chapel. Everyone wept noisily throughout the ceremony. I was the only person who spoke a word, and I nearly broke down.'

On occasions like these, one thanks God for the words of the liturgy. Without them, one would be speechless. In front of the minister is a dead child, who has not yet had a chance to do or achieve anything – all was promise, then there was nothing. And there is a mother, whose body quite possibly is still telling her that there is a life inside her, a life that only she had known for the nine months or more before the birth. There is nobody at the Funeral of a child wanting to say 'thank you'; everybody there wants to say (at the very least) 'why?'

Common Worship makes special provision for the Funeral of a child. There is an outline order rather than a full rite, and a significant number of helpful prayers and resources. The main difference between the outline order for an adult and for a child is the suggestion that the child's coffin may be in place before the congregation arrives. To do this often removes one of many unbearable strains from the gathering. If a parent desires to bring in the body of his or her own child, that could be done before the service, though this is more difficult when the place of the Funeral is not the local church.

The words for introducing the service (Resources for the Funeral of a Child) set the scene for a service where no 'answers' are proposed and no guilt is apportioned. There is affirmation that death is not the end, and that God cares as a loving parent for the dead child.

We have come together to worship God,
to thank him for his love,
and to remember the [short] life on earth of N;
to share our grief
and to commend *him/her* to the eternal care of God.
[We meet in the faith that death is not the end,
and may be faced without fear,
bitterness or guilt.]

(p. 301)

One of the recurring images is that of the comfort of dying in the embrace of God. It is an image that could help on two levels – the dead child can be trusted to the 'arms of God', and those who mourn can themselves find comfort in God's embrace.

One of the questions that may need to be faced with a miscarriage, stillbirth or very early death relates to the question of dying unbaptized (see the 'Theological Note', pp. 316–17). Each minister will have their own 'answer' should the question be raised, but the special texts do not discriminate between the baptized and the unbaptized. Rather, God is proclaimed as one who loves all whom he has made.

Most ministers would probably want to keep the service very short and uncluttered. Today it is more likely than formerly that there will be children among the mourners. If there are, special consideration should be given to them. The minister may wish to offer brief remarks, or readings or prayers especially for their benefit at various points through the service. The language of most of the prayers and texts is deliberately straightforward, while not sacrificing theological integrity. There are some prayers for the children in the family. Sometimes it can be helpful to involve the children present in practical ways; at other times that would only make the whole service feel more unbearable. A sermon is 'required', but difficult. There are some good children's stories about dying and death – these can be quite a helpful resource, and not just for the children present. (See Appendix: Recommended Reading.) Children can also, and perhaps more easily, be involved at home, in preparing, for example, for the refreshments at home afterwards.

There are related occasions for which a minister might need to offer a form of service if not a full Funeral. For example, in the case of a miscarriage where there is no body, there are prayers and readings in the *Common Worship* resources that could be adapted for a special service for parents (the mother in particular) who have been bereaved in this way.

There is also the possibility, if a child of school age has died, that the minister may need to lead an informal act of worship for the school. There are some prayers in the *Common Worship* 'Resources for the Funeral of a Child' that would help in creating such an act of worship. The outline order for the Funeral could well be adapted for such a purpose. Music and singing and responsive prayer might play a more important part. And if the service takes place in school, the children could be actively involved, perhaps in creating something like a prayer 'tree', or a cross of flowers, real or cut out, which could be placed either on the grave, or in church in memory of the dead child. (Activities such as these draw in teachers. On occasions like this, minister and teachers can act as helpful resources for each other.)

Violent or sudden death

The Funeral service for someone whose death has taken place in violent or sudden circumstances, or for someone who has taken her or his own life, obviously requires especial pastoral sensitivity. These circumstances have been taken into account in the prayer resources, where the composers have clearly worked hard to find the right words. It does matter enormously to those who mourn such a death that the situation is addressed in the words of the service and not bypassed.

Some families are aware of the past traditions of the Church with regard to Funeral services for suicides, and there is often a fear that a minister may refuse to conduct such a service. Canon law has problems only with those who take their life while 'of sound mind', and even then tempers its prescriptions by phrases such as 'may be'. Today, with all our knowledge of psychological illness, ministers are more likely to be thankful for suitable prayers than concerned about whether or not they ought to conduct a service.

The unbaptized

In a service for someone who has died unbaptized, we should use only those symbols and prayers that speak truth to the mourners. Some of the optional symbolic gestures in the *Common Worship* Funeral rites are exclusive to the baptized. The body or coffin of someone who has not been baptized should not, for example, be sprinkled with water or covered with a pall. The sprinkling with water specifically relates to the baptism of the departed (see text in Before the Funeral: Receiving the Coffin at Church before the Funeral. The pall is traditionally a baptismal garment (see Symbols, above), though the words in *Common Worship* do not make this very clear.

There are other symbolic ways, however, of expressing the Christian's trust in God's merciful love for everyone. The Paschal Candle, for example, which is also used at baptism, symbolizes the light of the risen Christ driving out all darkness of heart and mind. As such it can be a sign for everyone of Christ's constant presence, enlightening the whole world and driving out the shadow of death.

What if a minister is asked to bury someone who has not been baptized? According to Canon B 38, 'Of the Burial of the Dead', it is

> the duty of every minister to bury, according to the rites of the Church of England, the corpse or ashes of any person deceased within his cure or of any parishioners or persons whose names are entered on the electoral roll of his parish whether deceased within his cure or elsewhere that is brought to a church or burial ground or cemetery under his control in which the burial or interment of such corpse or ashes may lawfully be effected, due notice being given; except the person deceased having died unbaptized, . . . in which case . . . he shall use at the burial such service as may be prescribed or approved by the Ordinary . . .

The canon does not forbid the use of the normal services nor the burial of an unbaptized person, it simply says that if the diocesan bishop has prescribed an alternative service, that service should be used.

The unbeliever

Occasionally, an Anglican minister may be asked to conduct the Funeral of someone who was an avowed atheist. Usually, the request comes from relatives who do not share the deceased's atheism. This can put the minister in something of a quandary. Canon Law makes special provision only for the unbaptized, the excommunicated and suicides. Some ministers, and families, may prefer that the service be held in a cemetery or crematorium chapel and for the remains to be interred there. On the other hand, the Church of England is inclusive in its burial laws; every minister has a duty to bury those who die 'within his cure'.

The minister's prime concern will be how to present a service in a way that honours the integrity of everyone involved, the deceased, his or her family, and the minister. It is a difficult challenge. The *Common Worship* rite was not created for this purpose. A minister who feels it right to respond to such a challenge, however, will find several prayers that do not assume the faith of the deceased, but which will help Christians who mourn the death of an unbelieving relation or friend.

Not just words

Great care has been taken to create strong Funeral services and good related resources that should respond well to the many and varied pastoral circumstances in which the Church exercises her ministry at the time of death. A 'good' Funeral is not just dependent, of course, on the texts of the services. Also extremely important are the 'presidency' skills of the minister leading the service, and the care that he or she takes to choose and use the right material in the right place at the right time.

6 Bereavement and beyond

Ministering to the bereaved

A major purpose of the new Funeral services is to undergird the caring ministry of the Church with worship and prayer. The new services and prayers address all aspects of the Church's ministry after a death.

- Worship material is required to support the bereaved, both before and after the Funeral.

- A church community in which clergy and laity minister together needs texts that positively encourage their collaborative approach to bereavement ministry.

- Collaborative ministry stems from a congregation that is caring and well cared for. The new prayers and services will need to build and nurture such a congregation.

- Positive collaboration between church, Funeral director and, on occasion, the staff at the crematorium adds to the overall quality of ministry to the bereaved. How can the new resources be used to promote this additional dimension of collaborative ministry?

Supporting the bereaved

After someone has died, those who are bereaved need to carry out certain practical tasks, not least the reverent disposal of their loved one's body. They also have to work through their own passage of grieving. The material in *Common Worship* supports the bereaved in all of this, from the moment of death and through the weeks and years that follow.

Immediately after the death

As soon as someone dies, a whole process of arrangements is instigated. Almost the first thing the relative will do will be to make a series of phone calls: to the doctor, the immediate family, the police perhaps, if someone has died alone, the Funeral director, and, if they are church members, to the parish priest or minister.

It is well worth clergy telling members of their congregations that they do actually want to be among the first and not the last to be called on. People are often reluctant, as they say, 'to trouble you'. It is, however, enormously helpful for the minister to be advised as soon as possible after a parishioner has died. The new services give an excellent prayer resource, 'Prayer when Someone has Just Died', for example, which is very effective. This prayer puts into words the incoherent desire of the bereaved person to 'say something' at the moment of death to their loved one and to God. Such a prayer also helps the bereaved person release the body of the deceased person into the hands of the undertaker.

A minister should advise the usual Funeral directors of their readiness to be called upon to say prayers before the body leaves the house. Many Funeral directors are very happy to co-operate with their local vicar in this way.

Joan, a church-goer, rang her local vicar shortly after her husband had just died at home. By the time the vicar arrived, the undertakers were already bagging up Jim's body, and Joan was in the kitchen. Joan, when asked, wanted to say a prayer with Jim, even though his body was already in its black bag. The men from the Funeral directors were very understanding. Joan and the vicar knelt down by Jim's body and the vicar said the prayers. Joan said afterwards how much it meant to her to be able to pray with Jim before he was taken away. The Funeral director who was invited to remain in the room was visibly moved and made no secret of his feelings.

The first visit

More usually, the first visit from the minister to the bereaved takes place later, and usually well after the body has been taken away. The relatives will still be in a state of numbness and shock, but may have begun to cry. They will already feel under pressure to start talking practical Funeral details with the minister straight away, but it can help if the minister is able to say a few prayers with the family first. The act of praying seems to still the sense of shock and panic, at least for a few moments. If the visit is paid on the same day as the death, then the 'Prayer when someone has just died' is still very appropriate, with its strong purpose of entrusting and commending a loved one into God's hands.

If the first visit to the family is paid a day or two later, the *Common Worship* prayers 'At Home before the Funeral' may be judged more appropriate. If there are children in the bereaved family, or when the deceased is a child, one or two alternative prayers can be found in the 'Resources for the Funeral of a Child' and in the more general 'Prayers for Use with the Dying and at Funeral and Memorial Services'. Children who are old enough to understand and grieve should be included in discussing and praying about the death from the beginning.

A useful resource for the minister or lay visitor is a prayer or worship leaflet that collects together a selection of the most useful *Common Worship* forms and prayers. Such a leaflet can be used with the family at the time, and also left for them to use privately.

Planning the Funeral

The pressure is always on the minister (and the family) to begin to think about the Funeral within hours of the death taking place, though it is not always wise or helpful to be rushed into a speedy Funeral. Planning the Funeral, however, is a practical task that relieves some of the emotional strain on the family at the time. It may be that the deceased has already given some indication as to her or his preferences for the Funeral. (See Chapter 7, 'Designing my Funeral'.) The relatives are not bound by the deceased's wishes, but usually find it helpful to know that their loved one would have wanted it 'done like this'.

It helps if the minister has brought a Funeral planning sheet to the visit. Planning can be begun in this first conversation, and the planning sheet left for the family to continue thinking about and filling in. Most families like to consult with each other before making final decisions, and an 'ideas' sheet helps them do this. This is also a good way to put forward various options relating to the Funeral that people might not know about but find helpful. (See the sample parish service and prayer leaflets in Chapter 7.) Some families will take the opportunity, if offered, to borrow a book suggesting suitable prayers, hymns and readings in order to help them make their choices. (See Appendix 1: Recommended Reading.)

On the day before the Funeral

A choice that may be available to a family is for the coffin to rest in church overnight, or at least for some hours before the Funeral. Being in church overnight might be especially fitting for someone who has been a regular church-goer or for someone whose death perhaps was particularly distressing. Sometimes too a family, knowing of the large numbers who plan to attend the Funeral, will value a time of quiet worship and prayer with the deceased before the social pressures of the Funeral. Prayers can be said with them either at the reception of the coffin or at some other time before the Funeral Service.

The *Common Worship* prayers 'Receiving the Coffin at Church before the Funeral' and 'A Funeral Vigil' can be adapted to suit the particular circumstances. This might also be an appropriate time for a service of Holy Communion. Suitable texts for such a Holy Communion service can be found in the authorized *Common Worship* material (The Funeral Service within a Celebration of Holy Communion).

If the deceased is to be buried in the churchyard, some of the relatives may like to come to church for a service or prayers before the Funeral after the grave has been dug. It can be pastorally very helpful to stand with the family around the open grave sometime before the Funeral service and say a prayer with them. The prayer authorized for the blessing of a grave (in the Supplementary Texts) can be adapted for this purpose.

On the day of the Funeral

Some families appreciate prayers being said with them (or prayers to say on their own) on the morning of the Funeral. The form given in *Common Worship* can be used as it stands, and it would be good to be able to leave a parish prayer leaflet containing these prayers with the family.

For those unable to attend the Funeral

A church-going family with Christian friends who are unable to attend the Funeral might appreciate being given a prayer leaflet to send on to them. The church could easily produce such a leaflet using the resources 'For those Unable to be Present at the Funeral'.

These prayers could be used informally or privately, or even take the form of a short act of worship led by a friend or family member. (Everything would need to be printed in full.) The addition of a few prayers for those who mourn would also help.

Returning home after the Funeral

When the deceased has left a widow, widower or other family members who lived with him or her, the first return to the family home after the Funeral can be a very traumatic experience. Some people may need help in coping with this. When a young family is involved, there is particular need for something to be said, not least for the sake of the children. People need to be reassured that it is natural to feel angry, or sad or depressed.

Prayers in the home, and especially in rooms closely associated with the deceased, can be extremely releasing. (Formal words and prayers are often less emotionally stressful than our own.) An imaginative adaptation of the prayers 'At Home before the Funeral' could serve this purpose well. (See Chapter 7.)

Some rooms may feel more or less taboo, and a special prayer in that room could ease some of the emotions that the family are feeling. It is not unusual for the dead person's room to be left undisturbed, at least for a while, and there is a consequent risk –

especially when a child has died – of its becoming a shrine. The reluctance to change things can inhibit the natural grieving process, and the consequences can be disastrous.

The Burial of Ashes

If a person has been cremated, the Funeral Service is not seen as complete until the ashes have been disposed of. The new authorized form is slightly longer and more satisfying than *The Alternative Service Book* form.

Occasionally, unusual requests are made.

'Father was a pilot in the war. It meant a lot to him. He wanted his ashes cast into the sea from one of the planes he used to fly.'

Provided what is planned is legal (and the above request was!), a minister could assist by offering a little prayer sheet, adapted from the authorized form, for a representative of the family to say at the time of the committal.

A Memorial Service

'We want a quiet funeral, please, and then a thanksgiving service a short while later for all his many friends.'

'We want Mother's remains to be interred with Father. Can we have a quiet cremation first (Mother died at a distance from where Father's remains are interred) and a 'big service' and interment with Dad later?'

There are all sorts of reasons why a family might want a second main service in addition to the Funeral Service. It might be something to do with needing to return to the place from which the family originally came, or with the fact that large numbers of people will want to come and the small parish church building is not able to hold them all. Sometimes family distress at a death can cope only with a very quiet and relatively private Funeral first. Again, it might be that the requirements of the memorial (thanksgiving) service are quite different from the requirements of the Funeral service. Whatever the circumstances, the outline order of the Memorial Service with its notes and suggested resources meets a very real pastoral need.

Annual remembrances, anniversaries and other occasions

Visiting the grave

Many bereaved people visit their loved one's grave regularly, and especially on anniversaries and major festivals. There are several prayers in the new material that might be helpful at such a time, including the ending prayers from the provision for Receiving the Coffin at Church before the Funeral. These prayers (or adaptations) might be included on a parish's leaflet of helpful prayers for the bereaved. The same prayers might also be useful when the memorial stone or marker is placed in position.

Special anniversaries

Especially in the first years after bereavement, significant anniversaries are particularly difficult. Birthdays, wedding anniversaries and Christmas, for example, as well as the anniversary of the date of death, are all times when the sense of a loved one's absence is especially acute. One way in which the church could help is by remembering the bereaved and their deceased loved ones in the parish prayers at the time of the anniversary and writing to assure the bereaved that they have been prayed for. Another simple thing that means a lot to people is the opening up of the pages of the church's Book of Remembrance to 'their' name on 'their' day.

All Souls' Day services

Increasing numbers of churches hold a special service each year on or around 2 November, All Souls' Day. All those people whose family Funerals have been held in the church over a certain period of time are invited. Regular church members will also value the opportunity to remember their loved ones in prayer, and the All Souls' Day service can become quite a highlight in the life of the parish. The service may or may not take the form of a Eucharist. A special Holy Communion service and a 'Service of Prayers and Readings' in Commemoration of the Faithful Departed can be found in *The Promise of His Glory*.

Enabling and resourcing collaborative ministry

The ministry team in a parish will increasingly include authorized lay ministers, such as Readers and Pastoral Assistants, as well as other caring lay people, all working collaboratively with the clergy. This means that there can be quite a rich resource for bereavement ministry in a parish. The *Common Worship* services and prayers encourage and make liturgical space for such a wide ministry resource.

In many cases, the Notes encourage the possibility of lay people assisting with some of the suggested services and prayers. In order to facilitate this wider lay ministry, many parishes are now encouraging, training and resourcing individuals and groups of individuals. The new services offer the opportunity for an expansion of bereavement ministry in our parishes, and those who exercise this ministry will rightly look for training to make the best use of these new opportunities, and for appropriate supportive literature. Something else, of course, that a group of such people might be able to do is to create support groups or networks where families who have experienced the death of, say, a child, in the past, can be put in touch with others currently going through a similar experience.

Between death and Funeral

Probably the first 'official' person from the church to visit a house where there has been a death will be one of the clergy, or a Reader if he or she will be officiating at the Funeral. Depending on the length of time that has elapsed between the death and the visit, either the 'Prayer when someone has just died' or the prayers 'At Home before the Funeral' would be appropriate.

When the person who has died has been a member of the church, one or more fellow church members may have been visiting him or her before the death. One of them may well be with the family either at the moment of death or shortly after. She or he may well be the right person to say the prayers with the family at the time of the death. Even if he or she is not present at the precise moment of death, the same prayers may still be appropriate later. A prayer leaflet would be helpful both for use with the family and to leave with the family for them to use on their own.

It is very important to honour the caring ministry of the laity when someone dies. Lay visitors often assume that when someone dies, the minister or priest is better equipped to 'take over' from them. This is not always true! But even when the minister does take on the central role with respect to the Funeral, there are many ways in which the collaborative approach to ministry can continue after the Funeral.

Planning the Funeral

The planning of the Funeral is normally done with the minister who will be presiding over the service. In some cases, the deceased will already have indicated their wishes concerning the content and conduct of their Funeral. It is extremely helpful if this has been recorded, and if the minister presiding over the Funeral knows about it and can share that information with the family. (See Chapter 7, 'Designing my Funeral'.) On occasion, a husband or wife (or another family member) will have pre-deceased the person whose Funeral is being planned. Knowledge of what was done at that previous Funeral often helps those organizing the current one. (Hopefully, parish office records are well kept and are easily accessible.)

Whatever the circumstances, a Funeral planning leaflet, for regular use in the parish, would be very helpful to those people who have to sort out the arrangements. Such a planning sheet might include wider practicalities as well as specific contents. The wider practicalities would relate, for example, to which service, where, when and how; and the specific contents of hymns, readings and prayers, music before and after, as well as to who, if anyone, might be giving a tribute or taking part in other ways. (See Chapter 7, 'Designing my Funeral'.)

Presiding at the Funeral Service

The role of the presiding minister is a very important one. The president has to lead the service well and sensitively. Everything has to be planned carefully beforehand. The president assists with the creation of good printed service sheets and consults with all the people involved in the service – the assistant minister(s), the organist, the churchwarden, the sound technician, the visiting preacher, as well as with those members of the family or friends of the deceased who will be 'doing something' in the service.

The *Common Worship* services have a clear structure, which is a distinct bonus when the 'order of service' sheet is being drawn up for the Funeral. Mourners notice even the smallest details, and frequently make comparisons between the ways different churches and ministers conduct the Funerals they attend!

Presiding at Funerals on one's own can be a lonely business. Many ministers appreciate sharing the leadership of Funerals with a Reader or one of their other authorized lay ministers. Such collaboration is mutually supportive. It is also very acceptable to congregations who, provided all is done well, welcome the wider breadth of care. The role of a Reader in the leading of Funerals is well established. We need to be a little more imaginative, however, at involving in the liturgy other members of the laity who share in the church's pastoral ministry. There is no reason, for example, why a member of the congregation who knew the deceased well might not lead the prayers at the Funeral.

After the Funeral

Increasingly, lay members of the congregation will exercise much of the pastoral bereavement care after the Funeral. The prayers 'For those Unable to be Present at the Funeral', or 'On the Morning of the Funeral', or 'At Home after the Funeral' may all be led by lay people. A parish ministry that is serious about encouraging and enabling such lay ministry will want to create their own parish pastoral material from the *Common Worship* provisions (cf the examples in Chapter 7).

Annual remembrances, anniversaries and other occasions

If the church's ministry team is going to provide the further bereavement care of remembering and responding to anniversaries, or setting up and inviting people to a parish All Souls' Service, then keeping an accurate data base is crucial. While this may well be administered by the parish office, one or more of the lay ministry team could helpfully focus it. A prayer card sent on the anniversary of the death, making sure that names are included in the church's prayers on the right day, all these and other 'little things' enrich the church's pastoral ministry. Prayer resources to support these aspects of care can be found in the collection of Resources and Prayers for Use with the Dying and at Funeral and Memorial Services.

Building up a caring and cared-for congregation

The Congregation

Pastoral care is not restricted to members of the church's ministry team, be they ordained or lay. Every member of the church, in many and various ways, expresses Christian love and concern for those who are bereaved. They send cards, write little notes, cook meals, say prayers, or give flowers.

This gentle ministry will happen spontaneously, though it can be supported by, for example, making cards and prayer leaflets available in church. Suitable prayers for private use could be included in the pew sheets each week. The prayers and intercessions in the church's services, where individuals and families are named, involve the whole congregation; so does, for example, a 'prayer requests' board or scheme.

If a church has a discipline of praying for the bereaved or the departed, on, say, the three Sundays after a death, or on anniversaries, families can be advised and invited. This also gives another opportunity for the congregation to express its loving concern for the bereaved.

An annual prayer 'diary' can be kept, possibly in a public place, so that anniversaries can be remembered. The church's Book of Remembrance might have a place here.

Occasionally gifts are given to the church in memory of people's loved ones. A short form of prayer, say at the time of the offertory, can honour this expression of remembrance and love. One of the prayers of thanksgiving for the life of the departed might well be adapted and used:

Father in heaven,
we thank you because you made us in your own image
and gave us gifts in mind, body and spirit.
We thank you now for N
and what *he/she* meant to us.
As we honour *his/her* memory,
make us more aware that you are the one
from whom comes every perfect gift,
including the gift of eternal life through Jesus Christ.

(p. 352)

Caring for the carers

Clergy, lay visitors and congregation

It is important to remember the needs of all those who care for the bereaved. A whole congregation can grieve for someone's death, and often does. The priest or minister can also feel bereft. Clergy and congregation alike should be able to allow each other to grieve, and offer support and care to each other. No congregation or minister should be ashamed to admit that one of the needs that must be addressed through the liturgical ministry of the church at the time of death is their own. The new resources offer much more scope for that aspect of our ministry than did the preceding ones.

The Funeral director

A crucial, though often underrated, member of the 'wider' ministry team is the Funeral director. A wise and fortunate church and minister will have developed good working partnerships with those firms of Funeral directors who most frequently organize the Funerals over which they preside. It does take time and effort to build up good relationships.

The introduction of *Common Worship* provides an opportunity for minister and Funeral director to meet and discuss the possibilities provided in the new material. Such discussion will also enhance a respect for and understanding of each other's ministries, and how each can complement and support the other. This mutuality could benefit everyone, and most especially the bereaved family.

A Funeral director needs to know, for example, how soon the minister likes to be involved. The sooner the minister is involved, the easier it is to work together to make arrangements that fulfil everyone's needs and expectations. The minister needs to understand the pressures under which the Funeral director works, and to acknowledge that they too have needs. Permanently 'working with death' has its strains and tensions. And there are times when the Funeral director will know the deceased, or the deceased's family.

There are different ways of addressing this, not least an initial conversation on how each perceives their own and the other's ministry. The new rites give an opportunity for such discussion. The director may well appreciate being given copies of the parish's supportive literature, possibly as part of a 'parish pack' for their Funeral directors. Additionally, the new rites also give the opportunity for minister and Funeral director to rethink together the presentation and content of Funeral service sheets.

In conclusion

The new *Common Worship* material serves existing liturgical, spiritual and pastoral needs very well indeed. It also opens up and resources new possibilities for worship, prayer and pastoral care. A careful and thorough study of all the *Common Worship* services and prayers (both commended and authorized) has real potential for enriching, reshaping and developing the ministry of the Church to bereaved people.

Bereavement ministry is not so much our Christian duty, as an act of love for all our sisters and brothers in Christ who pass through death and bereavement. It might be good to celebrate this shared ministry of love and care by adapting some of the *Common Worship* prayers for members of the pastoral team to use.

> Almighty God,
> you love everything you have made
> and judge us with infinite mercy and justice.
> We rejoice in your promises of pardon, joy and peace
> to all those who love you.
> In your mercy, bless us, as we seek to work with you
> to turn the darkness of death into the dawn of new life,
> and the sorrow of parting into the joy of heaven.
>
> *(Adapted from Prayer 24, 'Prayers for Use with the Dying and at Funeral and Memorial Services', p. 353)*

7 Creating our own resources and special services

> 'Thank you for leaving that prayer leaflet when you left. I kept looking at it all the time I was sitting with Mum. Peter and I used it to say prayers together with Mum before we went to bed and left her with the nurse. Can I keep it?'

Common Worship in the parish

The Funeral Services and related material are printed all together in the one *Common Worship* volume: Pastoral Services. The book also contains the Marriage Service, Thanksgiving for the Gift of a Child and the services for Wholeness and Healing.

Many parishes, however, will want to produce their own literature to address the particular requirements of their parochial situation. In these days of increasing computer sophistication, the production of such printed material is relatively easy. The content of the booklet can be selected in order to match the ministry requirements of the parish, and there is ample opportunity for creativity in design.

All *Common Worship* material is available in electronic as well as paper formats, on floppy disk (text only), in *Visual Liturgy*, and on the Internet (free of charge). Useful advice and tips on the secrets of producing attractive, well-designed service and prayer leaflets can be found in *Producing Your Own Orders of Service*, by Mark Earey (*Praxis*/Church House Publishing, 2000).

The following suggestions for printed pastoral resources have already proved helpful in some pastoral and parochial situations.

A Funeral planning sheet

The leaflet, 'Designing my Funeral' (see overleaf), has been in use amongst the congregation at Sheffield Cathedral for some time. The contents are reproduced here with the kind permission of the Dean of Sheffield, the Very Revd Michael Sadgrove, who first developed the leaflet with a Lent group at Alnwick who were exploring death and bereavement. 'You need to emphasize that it has no legal force whatsoever,' he wrote, 'and I always recommend that people don't fill it in "cold" but in conversation with their parish priest.'

Designing my Funeral (Sheffield Cathedral)

Name ....

Year of birth ....

Address ....

Telephone Number ....

Note: this form has no legal force. However, your next of kin will obviously wish to respect your wishes about your funeral service, so it is important that they know where a copy of this form is to be found in the event of your death. It will be a good idea to discuss your proposed arrangements with them, so that they are not taken by surprise amid the confusion and distress of bereavement. You should also deposit a copy of this form with the Precentor, so that it can quickly be found when arrangements need to be made. If you subsequently change your mind, and fill out a new form, make sure that the old one is destroyed. The Precentor will be very pleased to help you complete this form. Please ask for her help and advice.

1.   Your next of kin (names, addresses, telephone numbers)

2.   Do you wish to be buried or cremated?

3.   If buried, where? If cremated, what should happen to the ashes?

4.   Is there to be a service in the Cathedral beforehand? Or a Memorial Service subsequently?

5.   What kind of funeral service? (i.e. a funeral-only rite, or a requiem eucharist?)

6.   Hymns (3) for the service (please give the *first line* of each hymn)

7.   Have you any particular choice of reading/s? (Biblical readings are already given in the funeral service, but you may wish to suggest your own; and they may include the

reading of a favourite poem, or piece of literature. If you wish to have a special reading at your service, please attach a photocopy to this form.)

8. Would you like any special music to be played or sung, before, after and/or during your service? (If so, please give full details.)

9. Would you like a friend/colleague/member of your family/fellow church member to take part in the service in any way? If so, how? (e.g. read a lesson, lead prayers, offer a short appreciation)

10. Do you wish to nominate the people who will bear your coffin? (If so, please give names, addresses, telephone numbers)

11. Other instructions for the clergy, funeral director, or next of kin

12. Anything about yourself that would help those responsible in preparing the service (e.g. brief life history, church involvement, interests etc.)

Signed ....

Date ....

If you have suggested names of particular people under questions 9 and 10, it is important that you should have asked them first, and obtained their agreement to take part.

Note: this form is reproduced by kind permission of the Dean of Sheffield, the Very Revd Michael Sadgrove.

Similar forms could be created for the use of the minister and the bereaved in planning the Funeral, and also for planning a memorial or thanksgiving service.

A Funeral Services resource booklet for liturgical ministers

Once the minister or the ministry team has decided upon the selection of Funeral and related services that they will normally use in their parish, it can be extremely useful to create a special Funeral services resource booklet for the convenience of the parish's liturgical ministers – clergy, Readers, etc. The booklet should contain the basic material needed by the ministers for the situations they have identified.

The great advantage of a 'local Funeral rites' booklet is not only that it is a lot easier to carry around than the full Pastoral Services book, but that it can contain the orders of service and the texts from *Common Worship* that are regularly used by the ministry team.

Such a service resource booklet might well include the following orders:

- an order for Receiving the Coffin at Church;

- a prayer for the Blessing of a Grave;

- the 'normal' pattern for the authorized Funeral service in church (with the details of sentences, readings, prayers and other options chosen to reflect the preferences of the minister and the ministry team). The normal pattern for a full funeral service at the crematorium will probably be fairly similar and so can be adapted from this;

- the alternatives for an interment in the churchyard, and for committal at the crematorium;

- a selection of additional prayers that would be generally helpful;

- the order for the Burial of Ashes.

A pocket pastoral resource booklet for the minister

Ordained and lay ministers may like to make a personal selection of the *Common Worship* prayers and short offices that best support their pastoral ministry to the dying and the bereaved.

There are many good prayers from which to choose.

Such a resource booklet can be of a size to keep in pocket, briefcase or car, and might include:

- prayers for those who watch with the dying:
  - some sentences and prayers to be said with dying people;
  - prayers for those who are dying;
  - prayers for comfort and encouragement for those who watch;
  - prayers to be said when someone has just died.
- ministry at the time of death – a personal selection of texts from the *Common Worship* provision, which might include:
  - a short selection of Bible sentences;
  - prayers of reconciliation;
  - a short Bible passage (e.g. Romans 8:37-39);
  - prayers to be said with dying people;
  - prayers for someone who is dying (e.g. opening prayer, act of faith, litany);
  - texts for the laying on of hands and anointing;
  - words for the administration of Holy Communion;
  - a commendation prayer and blessing.
- some prayers for those who mourn;
- possibly some additional prayers of entrusting and commending;
- some prayers for readiness to live in the light of eternity.

Prayer leaflets

Sections from such a pastoral resource book could be photocopied separately and used in a variety of ways. Two examples of helpful leaflets might be:

- **Prayer leaflet for those who watch with the dying**

- **Prayer leaflet for bereavement visitors**

Those who watch with the dying – family and friends as well as lay ministers – will find helpful prayers to include in such a leaflet from 'Prayers for Use with the Dying'. Bereavement visitors could be helped by material in the Resources section: 'Prayers for Those who Mourn'; 'Prayers for Readiness to live in the Light of Eternity'; 'Prayers of Entrusting and Commending'.

- **Prayer leaflet that could be sent to mourners who are unable to attend the Funeral**

- **Prayers that could be said at home before the Funeral and/or on the morning of the Funeral**

One or two short 'acts of worship' for each of these situations could be created from the *Common Worship* 'At Home before the Funeral' and 'On the Morning of the Funeral' provision.

- **Prayers for those returning home after the loss of a loved one**

There is provision in *Common Worship* for a service that may be used at home after the Funeral. It would be helpful for both lay and ordained ministers to consider how they might like to conduct such a service, and then adapt or add to the *Common Worship* provision accordingly. One possibility might be to base this service on a 'blessing of a house' model, where the minister and family, having come through the door and said a prayer there, visit various significant rooms in the house, reading a short Bible passage and saying an appropriate prayer in each one, and then perhaps ending up in the kitchen or dining room with a prayer over a cup of tea or whatever. The concluding prayers could then be said when the minister leaves the house.

- **Prayers for special occasions**

A collection of prayers could be created from the *Common Worship* resources (possibly with some adaptation) in order to give to the bereaved after the first six or eight weeks of bereavement. This could include prayers chosen from the Resources section that might be said

  - when revisiting the grave;

  - on the anniversary of the death;

- on special anniversaries, such as birthdays.

A few additional prayers for help through difficult times and days could also be included.

Sample services

The Funeral Vigil and the Memorial Service offer scope for creating worship that is personally appropriate to the deceased and to his or her family and friends. The suggestions that follow simply indicate two possible ways of using the *Common Worship* service orders and texts.

1. A Vigil Service, at home, before the Funeral

This service was created from the *Common Worship* material when an adult church member died suddenly and unexpectedly. Several of her immediate family members belonged to the same church. On an evening visit between the death and the Funeral, therefore, after discussing and agreeing the Funeral arrangements, the minister led a short time of prayer and reflection based on resources from the *Common Worship* Funeral Vigil service. All present were more comfortable with relatively formal and traditional worship. Only the minister had a copy of the text, but it was passed round so that everyone read something.

The theme chosen was 'An Unexpected Death'.

- The gathering prayers were said as printed.

- One candle was lit.

- The first lesson was read: Wisdom 4.7-10 (not 8-11).

- Someone read Psalm 6 and the psalm prayer.

- A New Testament lesson was read: 2 Corinthians 4.7-15.

- Everybody said the Nunc Dimittis from memory.

- The Gospel passage was read: Luke 12.35-40.

- The minister chose a suitable prayer and gave a formal blessing after all had said the Lord's Prayer.

2. A Memorial or Thanksgiving Service

This service was held for an adult church member fairly soon after the Funeral service. The tradition of both church and family was 'traditional, middle of the road'. The congregation included family members who attended the Funeral, together with church and community members who did not attend the Funeral. The reason for arranging such a service as well as the Funeral service was to honour the wider service and networks of the deceased. It was a fairly formal service; family members chose the hymns and the readings.

The service consisted of:

- a processional hymn
- gathering prayers, the second of which enlarged on the prayer given in the sample memorial service
- a New Testament reading (chosen and read by a family member)
- two short non-biblical readings (chosen and read by family members)
- a 'family' tribute
- a hymn
- a sermon (given by the minister)
- prayers: the first prayer the one printed after the sermon in the sample memorial service; two prayers from *Common Worship* resources; two prayers from other resources
- a hymn
- one of the alternative authorized commendations
- The Lord's Prayer
- a hymn
- final prayer, blessing and dismissal.

Contemporary Funeral ministry

One of the distinctive features of the *Common Worship* Funeral provision is the abundance of choice that is now available. The choice extends not just to the texts of the service but also to the ethos of the occasion. It is still possible to conduct a relatively standard Funeral service. But for those who wish to work towards creating a special Funeral service for each unique individual who dies in the parish, there is now much more scope. It does take extra planning time, but the resulting services are appreciated. And the *Common Worship* outline orders, together with the given structures for the Funeral service, ensure that there is a 'common' feel to each service, however special.

The encouragement to be 'special' serves all Funeral opportunities well, not just the Funeral Services for church members. There may even be particular benefits for the Funeral Services we conduct for those on the edge of the church. There is a greater need to get to 'know' the person for whom we are conducting the service, which is bound to enhance the quality of our pastoral care for their families.

What is important in Funeral and bereavement ministry is to create worship that honours God and expresses Christian faith but is also true to the person who has died. The *Common Worship* Funeral material offers a clear structure, a good choice of texts and a variety of opportunities. It has the potential to serve the Church of England well through the early years of the twenty-first century, provided, that is, her clergy and lay ministers have the courage and sincerity to work with the wider range of possibilities and to make its vision their own.

Conclusion

The *Common Worship* Funeral provisions offer a succession of services and prayers to help people travel from the time of final illness, through the moments of commendation and death, into the early stages of bereavement. The resources give good support to the local churches and their ministry teams for the pastoral work of helping people come to terms with dying, death and bereavement. There is a clear acknowledgement of and response to peoples' fears and feelings about death.

The new provisions also proclaim strongly, in word and symbolic action, the Church's Easter faith. The many and various services and prayers resource the Church of England well for its spiritual ministry to the dying and the bereaved, as it affirms their Christian hope, comforts them in their grief, and encourages them with the promise of Christ's undying presence with them, and theirs with him, in this world and the next.

Appendix I

Recommended reading

The Funeral Services of the Church of England

The Book of Common Prayer

Burial Services (Alternative Services Series 1), SPCK, 1966.
These services have now been authorized for use until 2005.

Common Worship: *Pastoral Services*, Church House Publishing, 2000
This volume contains all the authorized and commended services and prayers.

Other Funeral Orders

Order of Christian Funerals: Vigil Service and Funeral Mass, McCrimmon, 1990
The current Roman Catholic services.

Collections of Readings, suggestions for Hymns, Prayers, etc.

James Bentley, Andrew Best and Jackie Hunt, *Funerals: A Guide*, Hodder and Stoughton, 1994.

Prayers, hymns and readings. The book contains encouragement and advice for bereaved people planning a Funeral service, together with good collections of prayers, Bible and other readings, lists of appropriate hymns and other music, and a useful index which helps with the selection of prayers and texts.

Cicely Saunders, *Beyond the Horizon*, Darton, Longman & Todd, 1990.

Prose and poetry that have helped the author face suffering and loss.

Martin Shawe (ed.), *Enduring, Sharing, Loving*, Darton, Longman & Todd, 1992.

An anthology reflecting people's struggles to accept the unacceptable – the death of a child.

Agnes Whittaker (ed.), *All in the End is Harvest*, Darton, Longman & Todd, 1984.

An anthology of themed readings, prose and poetry, known to have been of help to bereaved people. A potential source of Funeral readings, as well as a book of comfort for the bereaved.

Ecclesiastical Law

Rupert D. Bursell, *Liturgy, Order and the Law*, Clarendon Press, 1996.

Describes and analyzes a wide range of legal topics in so far as they impinge upon church services. Includes ministry to the sick, and Funerals.

The Canons of the Church of England, 6th edn, Church House Publishing, 2000.

Canons B 37 and B 38 relate to the ministry to the sick and the burial of the dead.

Liturgy and Pastoral Care

Martin Dudley (ed.), *Manual for Ministry to the Sick*, SPCK, 1997.

A useful collection of services and prayers from various sources for ministry to the sick. Contains some helpful and succinct guidance on various aspects of the rites, including 'how to' anoint, lay on hands, communicate the sick, etc.

John H. Westerhoff and William H. Willimon, *Liturgy and Learning through the Life Cycle*, Seabury Press, 1980.

A general guidebook which relates the worship of the church to its pastoral context. Useful short chapters on ministration to the sick, ministration at the time of death and the burial of the dead. American Episcopalian and United Methodist context.

Revising the Worship of the Church of England

Michael Perham (ed.), *Towards Liturgy 2000*, SPCK/Alcuin Club, 1989.

Interesting to read today the short chapter on the Funeral Liturgy and compare the suggestions with what we now have in *Common Worship*.

Worship and Theology

Christopher Cocksworth, *Prayer and the Departed*, Grove Books, 1997.

An evangelical liturgist asks whether we can find ways of expressing our prayer in relation to the departed which are faithful to the central concerns of catholicity and to the priorities of evangelical faith.

John A. T. Robinson, 'Learning from Cancer' (Sermon preached October 1983), *Where Three Ways Meet: Last Essays and Sermons*, SCM Press, 1987.

Children and Death

Elcanor D. Gatcliffe, *Death in the Classroom*, Epworth Press, 1988.

A resource book for adults who help children and young people come to terms with death.

Jeremie Hughes, *Will my Rabbit go to Heaven?*, Lion, 1981 and 1988.

Questions children ask, including questions about death, heaven and hell – and some answers.

Books for Children about Illness, Ageing and Death

Nicholas Allen, *Heaven*, Hutchinson, 1996.

Heaven can mean different things to different people – and dogs. Pictures and story for eight-year-olds and under.

Althea, *When Uncle Bob Died*, Dinosaur, 1982.

Explores the facts of death, grief, and fear. No faith aspect. Five years and above.

S. Hollins and L. Sireling, *When Dad Died*, Silent Books, 1989.

Tells the story of the death of a parent in a simple but moving way. Evocative pictures. No faith aspect. Simple text, but the realism could help older children and young adolescents.

Bill Merrington, *The Hideaway: A Book for Children who Grieve*, Kevin Mayhew, 1998.

A 'warm, engaging story' of a boy who has to come to terms with the death of his mother. Questions to think about, and written from a Christian perspective. For 10- to 14-year-olds.

C. Nystrom, *Jenny and Grandpa*, Lion, 1988.

What is it like to be old? Explores ageing rather than death. Mentions God. Eight years and above.

Doris Stickney, *Water Bugs and Dragonflies*, Mowbray, 1984; New edn., 1997.

Explaining death to children via the natural life cycle of water bugs and dragonflies.

Hans Wilhelm, *I'll Always Love You*, Picture Knight, 1985.

Story about a boy having to come to terms with the death of his dog. Four- to eight-year-olds. No faith aspect.

Books about Death and Bereavement

Rosemary Dinnage, *The Ruffian on the Stair: Reflections on Death*, Penguin, 1990.

A collection of personal stories – how different people understand and handle the fact of death. Enables reflection on how the Funeral service might relate to the different ways in which individuals respond to death.

Creating our own Service Books

Mark Earey, *Producing Your Own Orders of Service*, *Praxis*/Church House Publishing, 2000.

Practical advice for those preparing local orders of service in the new era of *Common Worship*.

Appendix 2

From The Canon Laws of
The Church of England

B 37 OF THE MINISTRY TO THE SICK

1. The minister shall use his best endeavours to ensure that he be speedily informed when any person is sick or in danger of death in the parish, and shall as soon as possible resort unto him to exhort, instruct, and comfort him in his distress in such manner as he shall think most needful and convenient.

2. When any person sick or in danger of death or so impotent that he cannot go to church is desirous of receiving the most comfortable sacrament of the Body and Blood of Christ, the priest, having knowledge thereof, shall as soon as may be visit him, and unless there be any grave reason to the contrary, shall reverently minister the same to the said person at such place and time as may be convenient.

3. If any such person so desires, the priest may lay hands upon him and may anoint him with oil on the forehead with the sign of the Cross using a form of service authorized by Canon B 1 and using pure olive oil consecrated by the bishop of the diocese or otherwise by the priest himself in accordance with such form of service.

B 38 OF THE BURIAL OF THE DEAD

1. In all matters pertaining to the burial of the dead every minister shall observe the law from time to time in force in relation thereto, and, subject to this paragraph in general the following paragraphs of this Canon shall be obeyed.

2. It shall be the duty of every minister to bury, according to the rites of the Church of England, the corpse or ashes of any person deceased within his cure or of any parishioners or persons whose names are entered on the church electoral roll of his parish whether deceased within his cure or elsewhere that is brought to

a church or burial ground or cemetery under his control in which the burial or interment of such corpse or ashes may lawfully be effected, due notice being given; except the person deceased have died unbaptized, or being of sound mind have laid violent hands upon himself, or have been declared excommunicate for some grievous and notorious crime and no man to testify to his repentance; in which case and any other case at the request of the relative, friend, or legal representative having charge of or being responsible for the burial he shall use at the burial such service as may be prescribed or approved by the Ordinary, being a service neither contrary to, nor indicative of any departure from, the doctrine of the Church of England in any essential matter: Provided that, if a form of service available for the burial of suicides is approved by the General Synod under Canon B 2, that service shall be used where applicable instead of the aforesaid service prescribed or approved by the Ordinary, unless the person having charge or being responsible for the burial otherwise requests.

3. Cremation of a dead body is lawful in connection with Christian burial.

4. (a) When a body is to be cremated, the burial service may precede, accompany, or follow the cremation; and may be held either in the church or at the crematorium.

4. (b) The ashes of the cremated body should be reverently disposed of by a minister in a churchyard or other burial ground in accordance with section 3 of the Church of England (Miscellaneous Provisions) Measure 1992 or on an area of land designated by the bishop for the purpose of this sub-paragraph or at sea.

5. When a body is to be buried according to the rites of the Church of England in any unconsecrated ground, the officiating minister, on coming to the grave, shall first bless the same.

6. If any doubts shall arise whether any person deceased may be buried according to the rites of the Church of England, the minister shall refer the matter to the bishop and obey his order and direction.

7. A funeral service at a crematorium or cemetery shall be performed only in accordance with directions given by the bishop.

Index